PRAISE FOR
The Resurrection of Mary Magdalene
by Jane Schaberg

A landmark work in feminist cultural and Christian testament studies.

—Elisabeth Schüssler Fiorenza

The most searching and passionately argued of the books in this category.

—*The New Yorker*

A giant leap forward in the study of this mysterious woman.

—Gail Godwin

If readers are looking for one book on the historical Mary Magdalene, this is the book they should read.

—Karen L. King in *The Women's Review of Books*

An extraordinary contribution to biblical scholarship and to the ongoing history of feminist revision of Western culture.

—Alicia Suskin Ostriker

Schaberg's book breaks new ground and is recommended for all libraries.

—*Library Journal*

This book offers a journey of intellectual discovery.

—Christopher Rowland

Schaberg has given students, scholars, and an educated public an unparalleled gem that will define Christianity and change the course of legend for years to come.

—*The Journal of Religion*

MARY MAGDALENE UNDERSTOOD

JANE SCHABERG
with
MELANIE JOHNSON-DEBAUFRE

continuum

NEW YORK • LONDON

2006

The Continuum International Publishing Group Inc
80 Maiden Lane, New York, NY 10038

The Continuum International Publishing Group Ltd
The Tower Building, 11 York Road, London SE1 7NX

www.continuumbooks.com

Library of Congress Cataloging-in-Publication Data

Schaberg, Jane.
    Mary Magdalene understood / Jane Schaberg with Melanie Johnson-DeBaufre.
        p.   cm.
    Rev. ed. of: The resurrection of Mary Magdalene.
    Includes bibliographical references (p.   ).
    ISBN-13: 978–0-8264–1898–2 (hardcover : alk. paper)
    ISBN-10: 0–8264–1898–8 (hardcover : alk. paper)
    ISBN-13: 978–0-8264–1899–9 (pbk. : alk. paper)
    ISBN-10: 0–8264–1899–6 (pbk. : alk. paper)
    1. Mary Magdalene, Saint. I. Johnson-DeBaufre, Melanie. II. Schaberg, Jane. Resurrection of Mary Magdalene. III. Title.

BS2485.S34 2006
226.092—dc22

2006029496

Printed in Canada on recycled paper

Contents

A Note to the Reader 7

Introduction: Magdalene in the Past and Future 9

1 A Dig of One's Own 17

2 Thinking Back through the Magdalene 32

3 The Woman Who Understood (Too) Completely 67

4 The Women Did Not Flee 98

5 Mary Magdalene as Successor to Jesus 127

Conclusion 152

Important Terms 157

Questions and Resources for Discussion 161

Notes 169

About the Authors 175

A Note to the Reader

Although *The Resurrection of Mary Magdalene* (Continuum, 2003) can be read by people who have not had extensive training in biblical and religious studies, we hope that translating it into *Mary Magdalene Understood* for non-specialist readers will bring even more people into conversation with each other about Mary Magdalene in history and tradition. To this end, we have added discussion questions so that the book can be fruitfully used in study groups and classrooms.

This shorter version of *The Resurrection of Mary Magdalene* is also a new book that stands on its own. We believe its combination of Jane's interpretations with Melanie's insights and editing have created a clear and persuasive argument for thinking about Mary as part of a movement and as a prophetic successor to Jesus. The "I" in this book is Jane's, carried over from her larger book. Melanie has enriched and clarified that voice, and has added framing, elaborations, and resources for the reader. Thus *Mary Magdalene Understood* is primarily a work of feminist collaboration. The book has also been enhanced by important feedback from others—the Rev. Martha Koenig Stone of Rochester, NY, Melissa Widitor of Pittsfield, MA, and Evander Lomke at Continuum International.

At least two things have been lost in this translation. The first is access to the rich and varied scholarly conversation about Mary Magdalene. We have provided a few resources to extend your study, but have removed the extensive footnotes and quotations appearing in *Resurrection*. If you wish to dig deeper into this scholarly conversation, we recommend that you consult the larger book in your academic work.

For us, the second loss is more profound. In *Resurrection*, writer and social critic Virginia Woolf (1882–1941) acts as a guide, interpreter, and intellectual companion on the journey in search of Mary Magdalene. In this shorter version she only haunts the pages, popping in now and then in the epigraphs or to comment on this or that. If you are intrigued by Woolf's voice and insights, you may want to consult chapter 1 of *Resurrection*.

All the conversation and controversy over Mary Magdalene shows that her story has become a place where people explore and debate their views of Christianity, society, and themselves. In this sense, what we say about who Mary Magdalene *was* closely relates to what we say about what Christianity *is* and *will be*. We invite you to join us in this important conversation about the past and to take up the crucial work of imagining the future.

Jane Schaberg and Melanie Johnson-DeBaufre
On the Feast Day of Mary Magdalene
July 22, 2006

Introduction
Magdalene in the Past and Future

> I am now & then haunted by some semi mystic very profound life of a woman, which shall be all told on one occasion; & time shall be utterly obliterated; future shall somehow blossom out of the past.
>
> VIRGINIA WOOLF
> Diary, November 23, 1926

BY NOW, THE MOVIE VERSION of *The Da Vinci Code* has hit the box office and once again people have wondered about who Mary Magdalene really was and why it matters. The talk about this mysterious and yet overexposed woman will not end with the movie. Mary Magdalene is far too big for Hollywood. The movies that actually have a character named Mary Magdalene see in her a mix of lust, loyalty, belief, prostitution, repentance, beauty, madness, and sainthood. Her character is often central and yet powerless; she is frequently silent yet speaks volumes with her eyes and her touch. Books have tried to contain her. Through centuries of Christian literature she has been ignored, labeled, replaced, conflated, diminished, and openly opposed. But she has always, also, been utilized, unsilenced, rediscovered, and resurrected, living again in new legends, ideals, and fantasies.

This book is about searching for the Magdalene of history. This can be a daunting task because there is so little information about her. And yet there are so many impressions of her—shaped by centuries of sermons and paintings, poetry and saints' legends, romance novels and Jesus movies. I used to think of all this as rubble that had to be cleared. Now I see, as the archaeologist does, that some stuff is rubble, some precious; a sifting is necessary. If you are willing to engage in the process of sifting, you can learn something about both Mary Magdalene and yourself, about one woman and about every woman's struggles to be heard, taken seriously, understood. If you don't care about women's history, or think all history is meaningless, or think Christianity and religion itself are unevolved, best ignored, I can't tell you why you should care about Mary Magdalene.

Sifting through the Rubble

This is a shorter and less technical version of my book *The Resurrection of Mary Magdalene: Legends, Apocrypha, and the Christian Testament* (Continuum, 2003). It provides all of the most important details needed to study Mary Magdalene in the Bible, and in history and legend. Like that book, this one builds on the work of many literary critics and art historians, biblical scholars and scholars of religion. It is primarily indebted to the work of feminist biblical scholars who have broken new ground and have created a field of research that has produced a rich harvest of insights, knowledge, and possibilities. In many ways, I see research on Mary Magdalene as part of the women's movement and its ongoing work.

In this book you will hear a range of voices and moods: there is the irritable, almost finicky voice of striving after "fact" and precision, of fascination with detail, of exhaustion. There is also the voice of puzzlement and reflection and bemusement and horror, like a reader talking back to an engrossing novel. But this book is not a novel. It soberly asks historical questions about origins, authors, intentions, and ancient meanings. However, it is not possible to be certain about past events, meanings, and intentions, and no scholar can be objective. For all of us, what we see depends on where we stand, and where we stand depends on who we are.

I am trained as a biblical scholar. This means that when I have a question about the past, I go first to the oldest data, the oldest texts. For someone who studies early Christianity, this often means beginning with the texts of the Christian Testament* (for this term and others marked with *, see Important Terms at the back of the book). But this book takes a different route. Chapter 1 begins, literally, in the rubble of Migdal, the site of ancient Magdala in modern Israel/ Palestine. Chapter 2 moves back through the Magdalene legends— from Hollywood movies to medieval saint stories. This approach invites you to sift things, take stock of where things are, why people think what they do about Mary Magdalene, and what difference it makes for how people think about women and men, sexuality, and Christianity.

Building on these insights, chapter 3 takes up the ancient texts— first, the ones that are not in the Christian Testament. Often called gnostic,* they present Mary Magdalene as a central character, startlingly different from her legends, praised and opposed as the woman who knew (too) much. The profile of Mary Magdalene from these texts seems at first to bear little relation to the biblical character from the four Gospels (Matthew, Mark, Luke, and John). It is common to think of the apocryphal* texts as late, as a branching out of the biblical tree. But both the Gospel image of Mary and the image of her in these other texts go down to the roots; their biology is interactive, radically symbiotic. Historians are learning that the differences between these ancient images of Mary give us a glimpse of the conflicts among different forms of early Christianity, especially those under the names of Mary Magdalene and the apostle Peter. Mary represents women's prophetic power both inside and outside the Christian Testament. The difference is how that power is remembered, evaluated, and managed.

Finally arriving at the canonical* texts, chapters 4 and 5 look at the Christian Testament through the lenses of their long and rich afterlife. This is not a bulldozing for some pure and authoritative version of Mary hidden under the rubble of the texts and legends. Mary's legendary afterlife can clue us in, give us a glimpse of what might have been going on when Luke changed the woman who anoints Jesus' head for kingship and burial in Mark 14:3–9 into a sinful woman who washes Jesus' feet and wipes them with her hair in Luke 7:36–50, and help us see the way that John 20 both remembers and diminishes Mary's spiritual insight and prophetic witness to the resurrection. Now we might see the social and religious vision of the *basileia* (or "reign") of God* that inspired Jesus, Mary, and others and that carried on in the name of Jesus after his death, as well as the contentious politics that have always intertwined with realizing such a vision.

Sifting through the rubble is important because the history of the harlotization of Mary Magdalene means that the Christian Testament texts that were actually about her have been and still are read differently through the lens of legend. Her witness is often seen as romantic, emotional, crazed; her influence regarded as inessential, insignificant, minor. Even some modern historical research seems to me tainted with the subliminal thought: Oh, so Christianity all depends on the word of a whore? Anything to avoid it all depending on her word, the word of a looney, a whore, or, in general, on the insight of any woman. Mary Magdalene is the madwoman—angry mad—in Christianity's attic. She was hidden there because of an open and not fully appreciated secret, and its implications, at Christianity's core: that the male disciples fled and the women did not.

Reading from this Place

I have lived in Detroit for many years. Being a biblical scholar in this place means reading among the deep and tangled structures of racism, sexism, poverty, classism, colonialism, and of the despair and courage displayed by those whom these structures have enmeshed. Despite my early efforts to get a "better" job, I am lucky to teach in a non-elite, richly diverse classroom, where some— many—of our students are the poor (or the nearly poor, the recently poor). I try to be a co-learner in the effort to expose strategies of oppression like "whiteness," and to recognize powers of resistance. I agree with another biblical scholar who said, "Interpretation of the Bible is justified only if it is a source for political and religious renewal, or it is not worth the effort. . . . If the Bible has anything to do with justice and freedom, biblical scholarship must be able to question those very structures of power and expose their injustice and destructive potential."[1]

Standing with Mary Magdalene at the cross and in Detroit is a challenge not to turn away from suffering or from the body. It demands a resurrection faith that does not make the suffering all right, does not become dull to injustice, does not desensitize compassion or fear of death, but leads instead to action. Mary Magdalene of the Christian Testament is the one who stands by the dying, wrongfully accused, executed. Unable to anoint at an empty tomb of the disappeared, she still did not cease to love the dead. She remembered. Simply there, she becomes the place, the location, not just the symbol of the God who is thought to abandon, but does not abandon. Each of us wishes for one like the Magdalene to go down with us into death, to stay with us to the end. I say this with cancer on my mind, and remembering those I did not stay with until the end, those I love who died alone. Reconstruction of Mary's story may help us to stay, not turn away.

I approach the topic of resurrection with trepidation and reluctance. These texts deal with a (perhaps *the*) foundational belief of Christianity, rooted in the belief of some first-century Jews. What is meant by such belief? And is it true? True for me? I do not consider it more sophisticated or intelligent or courageous to dismiss these questions. But this is something scholars rarely talk about, unless they are up-front explicitly orthodox Christians. My own experience draws me to thinking about death and life. I belong to a group of survivors "privileged" to experience my mortality: first as a young child with a heart valve problem, then in my forties with Stage 3 breast cancer. All I remember about the latter experience is the terror of death, the striving to beat death, the will to live, the love of life. Having had to face that fear brought me no closer to an articulated faith, but only sometimes to the grasping of mantra-like phrases ("now and at the hour of our death") and to the presence and support of good friends. Nothing more, nothing less.

My mother, a lifelong Catholic who could be more cynical and disinterested in religion than my atheist father, was dying of emphysema. One evening we got into a conversation on a subject we had never discussed before. She asked me if, in light of all my work, I believed in life beyond death. "Do you believe that any of it is true?" Surprised and somewhat embarrassed by such a question, I stuttered something about not knowing, but hoping it was true. I stuttered something about apocalyptic.* I am ashamed—or something like that—of my stuttering answer. This book is in some ways an attempt to continue that conversation. But too late.

I think that the heart of resurrection faith is a belief in God's ultimate concern with justice for the whole person, for the body, and for the whole human community. My proposal is simple. In making the claim that God raised Jesus, Mary Magdalene was prob-

ably in earnest and not insane, not a liar. She was speaking and thinking and creating out of her own experience in the apocalyptically oriented *basileia* movement, and her experience of the execution of Jesus, and out of what can be called insight or inspiration. Whether one accepts this claim as true or not depends on how it is understood and whether it can be experienced in one's own life in any way.

You might ask if I believe in the resurrection of the dead? Yes, actually, I do. I also know that I will die. Resurrection is for me a "broken and living myth," as one scholar calls it, an outrageous hope grounded in belief in the God who gives life to the dead.[2] It is grounded in the invigorating, stubborn moments of struggling against multiple aspects of oppression *and* against self-righteousness. Scientific knowledge, in my opinion, makes this faith no more outrageous than it was in past ages when people were intimately acquainted with the stink and rot of death, and with injustice. Across centuries and across a lifetime, changing attitudes toward the body, sexuality, selfhood, death, and love influence understandings of resurrection. However absurd the notion of resurrection seems, writes another scholar, "it is a concept of sublime courage and optimism. It locates redemption there where ultimate horror also resides—in pain, mutilation, death, and decay."[3]

You might also ask how I understand my own Catholicism. I do not deny being a Catholic, or an American citizen for that matter, as long as I continue to benefit from the wealth of either institution, and as long as I responsibly, even loyally, oppose their institutional injustices. For the past forty years, official Catholicism has met the worldwide women's movement with misogyny and fear, the hierarchy and clerical culture of the Church has walled itself up in a tower leaning to the right. I do not underestimate its power to intimidate, to destroy work, and to harm spirits, consciences, bodies, peoples.

At the same time, looking beyond church hierarchy, it seems to me that Christianity is in the throes of a second Reformation, more extensive, more profound than the first. Catholics in high percentages disagree with official church teachings on contraception, abortion, ordination of women, and homosexuality. Hierarchical clout proves unable to silence dissenting voices. The "official" Roman Catholic Church, increasingly seen as patriarchy writ large, hideously boring, pits itself against egalitarian, communal realities and needs, and against the progressive dimensions of its own history. My faith and my hope rest in and are part of this dissent, this reform.

Reading from Your Place

This book is an invitation and an opportunity: an invitation to think about and with Mary Magdalene from your own place or perspective, an opportunity to have the data at your finger tips and some ideas, analysis, and questions to stimulate your thinking. Perhaps your interest in Mary is sparked by the popular discussion of her in novels and movies. Maybe you are a college or seminary student who is studying the Magdalene tradition in the context of a Christian Testament class or a course on women in religion. You may be part of a church study group or a local reading circle. Regardless of your location, embark on the journey with companions, be they members of a discussion group or other intellectual and religious conversation partners that you have encountered in your own life. For it is in our conversations and in our collective discoveries that we re-imagine both the past and the future.

CHAPTER 1

A Dig of One's Own

> And I thought how unpleasant it is to be locked
> out; and I thought how it is worse perhaps to be
> locked in.
>
> VIRGINIA WOOLF
> *A Room of One's Own*

"ENTRY FORBIDDEN," reads the blue and white sign. Snarling
watchdogs are on patrol; bales of hay are stacked high, covered with
plastic sheets. A stone house stands empty. This is Magdala, or Migdal, on the western shore of the Sea of Galilee, the town of Mary
Magdalene. It is marked only by a rusty road sign, stating that this
was the birthplace of Mary Magdalene. An undated, popular guide-
book called *The Sea of Galilee and Its Holy Sites* claims that "a small
white-washed dome near the road is a reminder of the meeting between Jesus and Mary Magdalene (Mark VI, 53)." But this is wrong.
The dome actually covers an old Islamic tomb, and no meeting between Jesus and Mary Magdalene is recounted in Mark 6:53. The
place is not mentioned in the major scholarly guidebooks.

Presently closed to the public, the archaeological site at Migdal
is surrounded by both an inner stone wall with chain link and curled
barbed wire on top, and another outer fence of barbed wire. There

are weeds growing over the dig that was directed by Franciscans—a dig which was suspended after five attempts (1971, 1973, 1976–77) because of a problem with water from underground springs. I have visited this place often since 1986 with students from the University of Detroit Mercy, and we joke about establishing an institute of feminist studies here, with no budget, no authorization, no permission even to enter. We joke about it as we try to find out *something* about the dig and even to get a decent look at it. It is "too dangerous, not possible" to enter, said Franciscan archaeologist Virgilio Corbo when we interviewed him at Capernaum in 1988. According to Corbo, the Israeli government forced him to stop the dig: there is water under the surface, and they are the only ones who can drain it. He said he suspected they really wanted to make a beach there.

The site is currently under the care of the family of Marwan Assadi and friends, who live in a small corrugated shack. Our taped interview with Marwan in the summer of 1989 was punctuated with loud bleating of a dozen sheep. We sat around a table in the shade in front of their home, eating chunks of watermelon and drinking strong coffee in tin cups offered with gracious hospitality. There is something haunting about the site. Surprised by my own question, I asked if there were any ghosts here. "Yes," said Marwan, pointing, "she sits over there."

On each subsequent visit, the place becomes more desolate and depressing from an archaeological point of view. The last time I visited, the sheep were gone, all sold, replaced by many chickens scratching up what is left of the mosaics. Certain stones I remembered were gone. The snarling dogs remained. Even with the connection with Marwan, who studied to be a truck driver and tells me he will call me when he comes to the United States, it is more and more difficult to enter because sometimes he is not there. What my photographs show, from year to year, is the scattering and sinking of stones, rearrangements, accumulation of trash—cigarette butts, plastic bottles. The green weeds and wildflowers are taking over fallen columns, pedestals, and low walls. Palm trees and eucalyptus trees abound. Graffiti is sprayed on the steel gate to the sea: "Do not go in, Do not go in" with the skull-and-crossbones flag meaning, "You can die here." Another sign with drawings of waves and palm trees: "Magdala Beach, History Place," but we never see anyone on this beach, and the history is mute.

But why am I, who deals with texts for a living, still trying to squeeze through the barbed wire? Why am I, who does feminist biblical studies, reading archaeology—a field seldom interested in feminist research and rarely of interest to feminist scholars? Why are we driving, then climbing up the cliff of Mount Arbel, which overlooks Migdal? Why are we sitting here on the edge of a sheer drop, in rebel territory, thinking of the ancient city and of present challenges? Surely this pilgrimage is like the relief parties Virginia Woolf led to ferret out the lives of the obscured, to rescue a stranded ghost. We are here to insist on the flesh and blood, the bone and rock of our own women's history. Our desire—impossible though it may be—is to connect over past time in present space with a real and historical forerunner.

The Rocks of Migdal

There is not much written about the dig at Migdal. Almost every aspect is confusing, including the recent history of the site. The Arab village that used to be here, called *Al Medgel* or *Mejdel,* was bulldozed by the Israelis in 1948. Nothing remains of that village but the Muslim grave. At the beginning of the twentieth century, a German architect named Lendle purchased land from the Arabs here and began excavating; I know of no reports of this effort. In

April 1935, two Franciscans, Saller and Bagatti, visited Mejdel as guests of Muktar Mutlaq, whose numerous descendants, born of his nine wives, made up almost all the population of the village. A little later, the Franciscans acquired property here, and the Italian Ministry of Foreign Affairs financed the digs. Today, the various claims to Migdal resemble the religious and political complexity of this part of the world. According to Rami Arav, director of the excavations in Bethsaida, the Franciscans own the small parcel of the excavated Migdal occupied by the Arab family, the Greek Orthodox Church owns another small piece, and the Jewish National Fund owns the rest.

The archaeologists faced great difficulties in Migdal, especially three: the reuse of materials over the centuries; the radical destruction by bulldozers in 1948, which aimed to wipe out all traces of the Arab village, and in the process pushed ancient materials toward the sea; and the underground water, always rising and returning. I think of the great difficulties of the Magdalene—the reuse of her tradition over the centuries, the textual bulldozing that aimed to wipe out all her traces, and the underground spring of her memory, always rising and returning.

The archaeologists did find a few things: on the northern edge of the dig, a large structure near the sea, possibly a Byzantine monastery, with badly damaged mosaic floors; and on the eastern side of the main road, several public and private buildings believed to be from the time of Mary—the first century CE.* One of these buildings may have been a first-century synagogue or a nymphaeum (a public fountain house). Some think this building was a small synagogue because it has five steplike benches (like bleachers) opposite the southern wall facing Jerusalem. If you enter from the west, the room looks like a small basilica or church with a central aisle and two aisles the length of the building. The building might have housed a small congregation, with room for perhaps 30 on the risers and 25 in the central aisle. There are no images or art in the building, which may suggest a Jewish congregation.

In the second phase of construction on the building, the floor was raised to the second tier of benches; under the floor was a channel for collecting water, and waterways ran between the three walls and the columns. Near the northern part of the building was an open court paved with large stones. Trenches on three sides collected water that flowed along a channel. The Franciscan excavators supposed that the synagogue was changed into a city fountain house or water storage building during the first century CE because springs of water flooded the building. Some scholars argue that it was always a well house, or the entryway to a villa, but there are no characteristics of a fountain—no niches, not even a fountain, only the water.

The archaeologists also found a tower, an aqueduct, a large paved court enclosed by colonnades, and an urban villa, probably built by a wealthy resident of Migdal. Its entryway had a first-century mosaic floor with the Greek inscription *kai su* ("and you" or "you too") and a square panel within which seven objects are represented in blue, red, white, and brown. Some regard these as magical symbols, and indeed the inscription—the only one of its kind found in Israel— may be some sort of invocation against the evil eye; the phrase *kai su* is known from private houses in Antioch in Turkey. Or, perhaps it is a quotation from a lost text called the Gospel of Eve: "*ego su kai su ego*" or "I am you and you are me."[1]

The seven symbols in the floor probably represent aspects of the fishing trade. There is a boat, in this case a five-person merchant sailing vessel used for crossing the lake carrying cargo. This type of vessel was developed to face the dangers of the Sea of Galilee with its sudden storms and change of wind direction. It is like the famous boat from the time of Jesus, discovered behind the breakwater at

Migdal in 1986 and preserved in a tank at Nof Ginnosar, about a mile north. That boat was worn out, stripped, and pushed out into the lake to sink beside a boat repair center at Magdala. A sailboat, we will see, turns up again in the legends of the Magdalene from France, but there it is rudderless.

The mosaic as a whole may illustrate the production and trade in salted fish to distant customers. There is a flower or bud lying on its left side between two leaves; two containers or baskets attached by a pole, perhaps for carrying loads on a pack animal's back; a large jar with two handles and a triangular base; and a fish head with a branch or piece of seaweed sticking out of its mouth. The villa owner may have been advertising the source of his or her wealth, or thanking God for it. Or perhaps this is not a villa at all. It could be a commercial building related to the fishing industry.

In what remains of Migdal, the Sea of Galilee is always present. Archaeologists found needles for repairing nets and lead weights to weigh them down. Migdal had one of the largest anchorages on the lake, with a breakwater enclosing more than an acre of the coast. Earlier Franciscan excavators did not realize that they were dumping their rubble into the ancient harbor. An examination of underwater structures based on an ultraviolet satellite survey from 1971 to 1975 shows that there was a wharf with a mooring stone for ships. A street constructed on the wharf lies more than nine feet under water. The port had a walkway that ran parallel to the shore and a sheltered basin; these outlines were clear and complete in the 1970s, but now the topography has been altered by rapid silting and development.

In 1991 when the waters of the Sea of Galilee were low after a severe drought, a tower appeared about 150 feet from the shore at Migdal. Stone pillars that apparently supported it were uncovered by the Antiquities Authority's Marine Archaeology Division, headed by Ehud Galili. Archaeologists believe that this was a lighthouse, for the fishermen working at night on the sea. It is now submerged again. I think a lot about that lighthouse. It reminds me of Virginia Woolf's book *To the Lighthouse*. She talks about how the light searches things out even amidst decay and neglect: "The place had gone to rack and ruin. Only the Lighthouse beam entered the rooms for a moment, sent its sudden stare over bed and wall in the darkness of winter, looked with equanimity at the thistle and the swallow, the rat and the straw. Nothing now withstood them; nothing said no to them."[2] Perhaps if we keep looking, we will catch a glimpse of Mary.

The Texts about Migdal

Sometimes it helps to look at the textual remains of a place, to read how the city is remembered in order to write its history again. Although the artifacts are few, texts that mention Migdal can inform our impressions. Not surprisingly, the city was well known for its prosperous fishing industry. The ancient geographer Strabo reports that in this area "the sea provides the finest fish for pickling, and on its banks grow fruit trees which resemble apple trees."[3] The Talmud mentions that the city had a small harbor and a boat-building industry.

As with most port cities, the town also had a reputation for opulence and immorality. According to the literature of the rabbis, "Magdala was destroyed because of prostitution," and because of the profound corruption of its inhabitants.[4] So strong is the legend that Mary Magdalene was a prostitute that some scholars have linked this reputation of the city to Mary's story and suggested that "Mary the Magdalene" might have meant "Mary the Harlot." Others ask if there is a correlation between Magdala's depravity and the seven demons cast out of Mary. Why are we quick to link the city's reputation for sexual depravity to Mary but we do not connect her to Migdal's reputation for fishing? Jesus, after all, did call his disciples from their boats, their nets, and their livelihoods in the fishing industry.

Or, why not read Mary through Migdal's connection to women's mystical traditions? The rabbis say that the daughters of Job died at Migdal Seb'iyah.[5] The book of Job says that in his latter days Job had seven sons and three daughters. "In all the land there were no women so beautiful as Job's daughters; and their father gave them an inheritance along with their brothers" (Job 42:15). In a Roman period text called *The Testament of Job*, the daughter's inheritance is a gift of three multicolor cords or sashes. When the sisters put them on, they can speak and sing in the language of the angels, and can see and celebrate the heavenly chariot come for the soul of their father.[6]

Legend has it that Jewish mystics from Safed centuries later claimed that they rediscovered Miriam's Well near the Sea of Galilee. It was said that water from the well could wake you up and help you read Torah clearly. This was the well of sparkling water, created at twilight on the second day of creation, said to belong throughout history to those who know how to draw its waters: to Abraham, Hagar, Isaac, and to Miriam during the Exodus. Nevertheless, the rabbinic tradition associates Migdal primarily not with women's mysticism* but with men's scribalism. The rabbis speak of a famous study house at Migdal, a famous scribe, Niqai, and the rabbis Isaac and Judan.

This is the way recorded history is—highly selective, male-centered, and obscuring of women's presence and contributions. In fact, most of the textual remains of Migdal are concerned with leading men and wars. The Jewish military general and historian Josephus says the city of Migdal was surrounded by a great wall that he built. He describes two grain markets, a large aqueduct system, a theater, and a hippodrome that could hold 100,000 men.[7] But Josephus's numbers are often wildly inflated and these structures have not been found. He writes also of "the residence of the nobles," from which he made a canal leading to the lake, in one of his action-packed escapes.[8] This may be the urban villa with the fishing mosaic.

As a site of military history, Migdal and the area around it ran with blood. Around 161 BCE,* supporters of the Jewish revolutionaries the Maccabees were slaughtered in the caves at Arbela by the Syrian general Baccides.[9] In 38 BCE, soldiers of Herod the Great slaughtered supporters of his rival Antigonus, who had taken refuge in those caves.[10] During the war of 66–74 CE, when Josephus was commander of the Galilean revolutionaries' army, he made the area of Taricheae-Magdala his headquarters and fortified it.[11] He says that 40,000 men of the city were on his side.[12] On the eve of the Sabbath, he mobilized 230 boats and overcame his pro-Roman enemies from the city of Tiberias, imprisoning 600 members of the council of Tiberias.[13] Migdal was a Zealot stronghold and refuge for rebels, until it fell to the Romans.[14]

In the great naval battle at Taricheae, 6,700 Jews were killed by Vespasian's army in 67 CE. The Roman general Titus, on horseback, led his troops along the lakeside and into the town, killing those who were caught there. He then launched a flotilla to defeat those who had escaped by boat. According to Josephus, "One could see the whole lake red with blood and covered with corpses, for not a man escaped." A stench hung over the region, and the beaches were strewn with bodies. The Jews were plunged into mourning, and the conquerors were revolted.[15] The emperor Vespasian, sitting on his tribunal at Taricheae, granted the rebels an amnesty that was hardly amnesty: he let them leave the city but only by the road to Tiberias.

In Tiberias they were led to the stadium, where 1,200—"the old and unserviceable"—were executed, 6,000 youths sent to Nero, and the rest—30,400 except for those of whom he made a present to Agrippa—were sold.[16]

Like other cities on the Sea of Galilee, Migdal was at the center of the productive and destructive encounter of cultures so prevalent in the time of the Roman Empire. It appears to have been a Roman city, with its geometric grid. The Roman passion for entertainment is represented by the theater and hippodrome, where cultural, class, and economic differences would have been prominent. Migdal was a place where Jews and non-Jews met, an urban center on the main road that ran from Philoteria at the south end of the Sea of Galilee, along the western side of the lake to fork north to Damascus. Its location "implies traffic, commerce, and the flow of ideas and information, including gossip."[17]

Pilgrims and Tourists in the Holy Land

A long and varied chain of gossip about Mary Magdalene has brought me here. Like a pilgrim, I return to Migdal year after year, driven by my fascination or obsession with the details of this dig. Christian pilgrim sources from the time of the Crusades say that in the fourth century Queen Helena, the wife of the Christian Roman emperor Justinian, traveled here too, and that she found the house of Mary Magdalene and had a church built on that site. But the early pilgrims are silent about this: the Bordeaux Pilgrim (333 CE), Egeria (381–84 CE), and Jerome (386 CE) do not mention Mary Magdalene's house. Neither does Willibald, who passed by the village of Magdala in the early eighth century. In the thirteenth century, under Muslim rule, the church was not destroyed but transformed into a stable. By the seventeenth century, only ruins are reported at Migdal. In 1871 Captains Wilson and Warren say they found "a heap of ruins" there.[18]

The pilgrim trail to Magdala has gone cold. The evidence is lost, or all but lost. Carted off, scattered. In the Studium Biblicum Franciscanum Museum at the Church of the Flagellation back in Jerusalem, you can see a few marble fragments decorated with a vine leaf, possibly from what may have been the mini-synagogue or fountain. There are also some Roman pottery and bronze objects from Migdal. The glassware room displays vessels from Migdal—goblets, bottles, jewelry, lamps, perfume bottles. Nothing is carefully marked. To the west of Migdal, up the Arbel mountain range in the modern town of Upper Migdal, archaeological artifacts probably from the Migdal dig decorate homes: a telephone rests on an ancient column in one yard, a wine press sits in another. Who knows what was ground up by bulldozers, pushed into the Sea?

Compare the ruins here at Migdal to what goes on seven miles up the road at Capernaum (Kefar Nahum), one of the most important Christian excavations and tourist sites in Israel/Palestine. There, a modern church was under construction for some years. Iron rods protruded from slabs of concrete; wood and metal scaffolding surrounded the structure; there were great puffs and snorts of dust made by the tractor: moving, removing, reconstructing, covering. Finally finished, the twenty-two-foot high church, supported on eight columns, now incorporates the remains of a fifth-century memorial structure of three concentric octagons, considered by some archaeologists to have been built over the actual house of the Apostle Peter.

The single large room of that house is plastered, and graffiti mention Jesus as "Lord" and "Christ." There are also etched crosses, a boat, and over one-hundred Greek, Aramaic, Syriac, Latin, and Hebrew graffiti from the second and third centuries. Some may mention Peter. Fish hooks were found between layers of the floor; pieces of broken lamps and storage jars were recovered in the room, but no domestic pottery. The reasonable but cautious conclusion has been that this "may be the earliest evidence for Christian gatherings that has ever come to light."[19] The pilgrim Egeria did visit this site in the fourth century and reported in her diary, "In Capernaum a house church was made out of the home of the prince of the apostles, whose walls still stand today as they were."[20] The modern church, like a space ship with eight rocket launchers, perches over the remains, which are visible though windows in the floor and from the outside. A huge carved panel proclaims: "You are Peter and upon this rock I will build my church and the gates of Hades will not prevail against it" (see Matthew 16:18). Four color charts depict the excavation in stages and from different views, and help the pilgrim-tourists read the ruins.

This oldest Christian sanctuary, contained in a fancy modern church welcoming the tour buses, offers a striking contrast to the barbed wire of Midgal, the sheep and chickens walking down its Roman road and through its paved court. The *kai su* inscription and the mosaic from Migdal of the boat and six other objects have been carted to Capernaum and put on display with a blue sign: "first cent. ad magdala." Here are the politics of archaeology: who digs where, and why, and with what money. One need not travel to the great Basilica of St. Peter in Rome to see the contrast in attention and honor paid to the two biblical figures of Peter and Mary Magdalene. There is no rivalry between the sites along the Sea of Galilee, because it is no contest. But there is open rivalry in the ancient gnostic texts, with roots that twist and turn deep in the Christian Testament, as we will see.

Like a lot of tourists, I want to buy things. I want to buy the site at Migdal (a middle-class American's crass solution) from the

Commissariat of the Holy Land (Dear Sir, If you have no plans for the site at Migdal, once excavated by Virgilio Corbo, would you consider . . .), or at least to lease it (Dear Jewish National Defense Fund, I would like to make a bid . . .). I want to make a video for the Biblical Archaeology Society: shots of the weeds and chickens, illustrating and voicing the loss of women's history (Dear Hershel Shanks, Would you be interested . . .). I want to negotiate with Marwan's family about their living space, to interest some university's archaeology department, interest the Israeli Department of Antiquities, interest some women's cooperative, some philanthropist, even some Franciscan archaeologist, and eventually—what? Have the dig resumed, expanded, done more carefully, adequately controlled, have the clear, informative blue and white signs and the diagrams, create a small museum of Jewish and Christian women's history.

A dig of one's own. A dig with results for feminist archaeology. I want to bring up the submerged lighthouse and restore the harbor. I want to open up the mini-synagogue, or fountain, or entryway— into which springs keep bubbling. Let's make use of all this information: expand it. Imagine the streets and buildings, the promenade and shops filled not just with Josephus strutting along with his men and mobs, not just male rabbis with their male students, but women and children and men, the elderly and the young, wealthy and poor, the marginal and the respected. A town with faces. Imagine the social dynamics of the fish industry and other businesses and technologies, the home, the synagogue. There would be a garden, a place to sit and commune with ghosts, to consider the agency of wo/men.* There would be a clean beach from which we and those who come after us could swim around the lighthouse, tie up our skiffs at the mooring stone. We could listen for the music of the daughters of Job, enjoying coffee and watermelon, and for the nonvegetarians, pickled sardines. In this artistic and intellectual community, all are at the table, in the discussion.

But no—in all likelihood Migdal will go further back into the earth, its artifacts lying there neglected or becoming the trash thrown out if or when a tourist hotel is built over it. A water slide; Muzak blaring; a huge plastic lobby; drinks with decorated swizzle sticks. Migdal will be a statement of what is lost, irretrievably lost to history, buried and overgrown and overbuilt, as the voices and actions and lives of the first century CE women are buried and overgrown and overbuilt by centuries of interpretation of the Christian Testament. Past events and historical persons, what really happened and who dead persons really were—I know these are irretrievable in any absolute sense. Certainty will always elude us. But the possibilities and the probabilities of women's historical contributions should be honored by examination, enjoyment, use, and imagination. And the lack of historical contributions, where that can be shown, should be described and mourned.

The ruins give us the chance to see both what is found and what is lost. There was an exhibition of photographs and texts about ruins held at the Getty Center in Los Angeles called "Irresistible Decay: Ruins Reclaimed." One of the curators, Salvatore Settis, writes, "Ruins signal simultaneously an absence and a presence; they show, they are, an intersection of the visible and the invisible. Fragmented, decayed structures, which no longer serve their original purpose, point to an absence—a lost, invisible whole. But their visible presence also points to durability, even of that which is no longer what it once was. . . . Ruins operate as powerful metaphors for absence or rejection and hence, as incentives for reflection or restoration."[21]

When we contemplate the luxury hotel that might or might not rise at Migdal, it seems true that ruins "persist, whether beneath the ground or above."[22] A short distance from the church at Capernaum, a ruin in its own way, Migdal's ruins persist in photographs, in memory, in curiosity, in sadness, in desire. Migdal is our irresistible decay, our necessary ruin. Migdal has no memorial, and is the focus of no reconstruction. The site stands for me as a reminder of loss, of the possibility of knowing nothing or nearly nothing. It is a reminder of distance, of the inexorability of time and death, of massive indifference and resistance. It teaches that even if we are convinced of wo/men's agency and power, even if we desire an ancestor of historical greatness, we may not be able to reconstruct our history convincingly; our reconstructions may be wrong. We have to be open to nothingness and disappointment. We are chickens scratching the remnants of mosaics. But still we scratch. I'll write it again. Migdal is our irresistible decay, our necessary ruin.

CHAPTER 2

Thinking Back through the Magdalene

> And when we are writing the life of a woman, we
> may, it is agreed, waive our demand for action, and
> substitute love instead. Love, the poet has said, is a
> woman's whole existence . . . (and as long as she
> thinks of a man, nobody objects to a woman
> thinking).
>
> VIRGINIA WOOLF
> *Orlando*

IF WE CANNOT DIG at Migdal, where there is "no entry," we can
scratch away at the legends. Clearing the site is preparation for the
work of chapters 3, 4, and 5, which examine the most ancient materials. In all four Christian Testament Gospels, Mary Magdalene is
a—perhaps *the*—primary witness to the resurrection, the fundamental data of the early Christian faith.

The Gospel of Mark says that Mary was with Jesus in Galilee and
then followed him to Jerusalem, stood by at his execution and
burial, found his tomb empty and received an explanation of that
emptiness (Mark 15:40–16:8). Two Gospels mention that seven
demons had come out of her (Luke 8:2; Mark 16:9). In three Gospels she is sent with a commission to deliver the explanation of the
empty tomb (Mark 16:7; Matthew 28:7; John 20:17). Those same

Gospels say she was the first to have a vision of the resurrected Jesus. Gnostic materials present her as a leading intellectual and spiritual guide of the early Christian community, as a visionary, the Savior's beloved companion, and an interpreter of his teachings.

My primary interest lies with these ancient texts. But for many contemporary readers, the Mary Magdalene passages have scrawled over them the word WHORE. Repentant whore. Whore who loved Jesus and was forgiven by him. This is the word many people today free-associate with the name Mary Magdalene. Her sexual "biography" has a long and varied history. Legends from the Middle Ages stress her penitence and apostleship; the Renaissance and Reformation, and nineteenth and twentieth centuries saw an interest in her role as a representative of female sexuality. Many recent Magdalenes—including in *The Da Vinci Code*—are created mainly to say something about the sexuality of Jesus, to save him from an asexual or (covertly) homosexual or purely divine image. Cleaning off the texts is an interesting task. It calls attention to the scrawling and the scrawlers of that word whore. This chapter examines how and when the Magdalene become a whore, and why.

The Image Distortion

No other biblical figure—including Judas, and perhaps even Jesus—has had such a vivid and bizarre life in the human imagination. If Mary Magdalene the Whore did not exist, people interested in the history of man's idea of woman would have to invent her, as complement and contrast to the Virgin Mother. Generation after generation has used her to explore fundamental questions concerning sexuality and the spirit, guilt and love. They have found their own thoughts in her, created her for their own needs.

Many people now know that the image of the Magdalene as a repentant whore is a distortion. And yet that image is still alive and powerful in contemporary novels, plays, films, and TV presentations. Take, for example, Robert Stone's journalist character Lucas, in *Damascus Gate* (1998), who muses about Mary in the creepy Holy Sepulchre:

> Mary M., Lucas thought, half hypnotized by the chanting in the room beside him . . . , the girl fom Migdal in Galilee turned hooker in the big city. The original whore with the heart of gold. Used to be a nice Jewish girl. . . . Maybe she was smart and funny. Certainly always on the lookout for the right guy to take her out of the life. Like a lot of whores, she tended toward religion. So along comes Jesus Christ, Mr. Right with a Vengeance. . . . Fixes on her his hot, crazy eyes and she's all, Anything, I'll do anything. I'll wash your feet with my hair. You don't even have to fuck me.

The themes of lust and love are always there. "I'll do anything," she says. Although they look different in different versions of her story, the themes are always the same.

In the historical novel for children, *Mary Magdalene: A Woman Who Showed Her Gratitude* (1987), Mary's story is told to promote positive role models for Christian girls. Now, the most prominent feature of the story is love: "Mary Magdalene was not famous for the great things she did or said, but she goes down in history as a woman who truly loved Jesus with all her heart and was not embarrassed to show it despite criticism from others." The tales of her lustful early life and repentance still take up half the book.

In Donna Jo Napoli's *Song of the Magdalene* (1996), the tale of Mary's early life is told in a way that resonates with the struggles of many women with poor health, poverty, and sexual slander. The young Mary has fits; she thinks of herself as possessed, filthy, and impure. But she learns better from her friend Abraham who has palsy, and who fathers her child before he dies. Mary's reputation as a prostitute is based on this pregnancy and on her rape by a man from her hometown, who slanders her as lustful. A man named Joshua prevents her from being stoned and she joins him in his travels. In this book for young readers, the whore legend shows that "if the Creator saw fit to ruin a woman's family—unless shelter was offered to her, unless work was extended to her, unless the community protected her—that woman, any woman, could become a prostitute. Any woman at all. Any one of us."

Tim Rice and Andrew Lloyd Webber presented Mary Magdalene in the 1970s rock opera *Jesus Christ Superstar* as a prostitute in love with Jesus but having an ambiguous sexual relationship with him. Obsessed and baffled by him, she massages and anoints him. In the stage and film versions, she is the foil for Judas; both characters sing "I Don't Know How to Love Him." In the 1988 Martin Scorsese film *The Last Temptation of Christ*, based on Kazantzakis's 1955 novel, it is Jesus who is obsessed and baffled by his connection to Mary. She is his "last temptation"—the temptation to be ordinary, sensual, domestic, fettered. As originally shot, the Scorsese film began with the young Jesus breaking his engagement to Mary, his decision forcing her, dishonored, into prostitution.

In Denys Arcand's film *Jesus of Montreal* (1989), Jesus gets angry at the institutions that sexualize and commodify women. In the film, a small troupe of professional actors performs a Passion play on church property. Their conflict with church authorities and the advertising industry leads to the cancellation of the play and the accidental death of the actor playing Jesus. Arcand gives us a sensitive and sweet-faced Magdalene who is not a whore, but whose sexuality has been exploited for profit: "I used to show my ass to sell soap and beer," she says. Jesus saves her from having to take off her clothes in a beer commercial. In a rage he overturns cameras, TVs, and tables, cleansing the studio. They kiss and she says, "I love you, you crazy nut."

Each film's Magdalene is the conflated figure of legend, the repentant whore. Barbara Hershey, who played her in *The Last Temptation of Christ*, speaks in a scary way about the connection of this conflated Mary to all women: "The thing that fascinated me about Mary Magdalene is that she represents all aspects of womanhood: she's a whore and a victim, a complete primal animal, and then she's reborn and becomes virginal and sisterlike. She evolves through all phases of womanhood, so it was a wonderful role in that way."[1] For Hershey, really *being* Mary Magdalene required her being very sexual. "My most important scene, as a prostitute in Magdala, was also the most difficult because I was going to show Magdalene with a series of men. . . . [Marty] asked me if I wanted a double, so at first I said sure. Every atom of me wanted a double. But I didn't feel a double would be Magdalene. I didn't feel she would move like I would move. I knew if I did the scene, I'd really feel like a whore."[2] Female sexuality is neither celebrated nor disdained in the film. But the viewer is not encouraged to see Mary, and women, as anything other than sexual. The image distortion is powerful and it gets repeated again and again.

Female sexuality and the feminine divine are claimed as positive albeit controversial elements of early Christianity in Dan Brown's novel *The Da Vinci Code* (2003), which rejects the image of Mary as a prostitute and creates a thriller-romance around the secret that Mary Magdalene was married to Jesus and bore his children, ancestors of the Merovingian kings of France. Mary is the "Holy Vessel [or Grail] . . . the chalice that bore the royal bloodline of Jesus Christ. She was the womb that bore the lineage. . . . Behold . . . the greatest cover-up in human history. Not only was Jesus Christ married, but He was a father." Why the cover-up? Because "the early Church needed to convince the world that the mortal prophet Jesus was a *divine* being. Therefore, any Gospels that described *earthly* aspects of Jesus' life had to be omitted from the Bible." Brown's book ultimately weighs in on an age-old Christian question about *Jesus*: What if he were human after all? This shifts our attention away from Mary again. In the end, she is still a vessel, a womb, a body part—no longer a prostitute, but now properly married. Has she been rescued, or covered up again?

The Da Vinci Code has resonated with people whose spirituality is not based in institutional authority and not based on denigrating human sex and sexuality. However, *The Da Vinci Code* ultimately reproduces conventional sexual stereotypes and male-centered expectations. The character Sophie (Mary Magdalene's fictional descendant) learns that the ancient practice of *hieros gamos* (sacred marriage) was a spiritual act that helped the *male* achieve spiritual insight and communion with God: "The ancients believed that the male was spiritually incomplete until he had carnal knowledge of the sacred feminine. Physical union with the female remained the sole means through which man could become spiritually complete and ultimately achieve gnosis—knowledge of the divine." Women's sexuality, in other words, helps men achieve their full spiritual potential.

I have found only one popular treatment of Mary Magdalene that refuses the temptation to shape Mary's story around sexuality, love, or lust. In *A Letter of Mary* (1996), Laurie R. King depicts Mary as formerly mad but not formerly a whore. An amateur archaeologist finds an inlaid box containing an ancient letter; it is from "Mariam, an apostle of Jesus the Messiah" written in haste during the destruction of Jerusalem in 70 CE. Mary Russell, Sherlock Holmes's colleague, decides not to release the letter until ten years after her death. "I suppose that the Christian world at the close of the twentieth century will be better equipped to deal with the revelations contained in Mary's letter than it was in the century's earlier decades." Unfortunately, the only bombshell the letter contains is the word "apostle." At the movies, only Arcand's *Jesus of Montreal* and Franco Zeffirelli's 1977 made-for-TV movie *Jesus of Nazareth*, to which I will return at the end of this chapter, contain startling images that threaten to break out of the legend.

The Conflation

Mary Magdalene became a whore in the historical imagination through a process of ignoring some texts and focusing on others. In the earliest centuries, it was accomplished through the conflation of several Gospel characters and stories. Conflation merges and strings together texts to make a kind of novelistic whole. The conflation of characters and stories can happen for several reasons.

Sometimes, conflation comes from confusion. Mary Magdalene is one of many Marys in the Gospel stories, all of whom are hard to keep straight. Jesus' mother was named Mary, as were as many as five other women associated with him: Mary of Bethany, Mary the mother of James the Less and of Joses, "the other Mary" (Matthew 28:1), Mary Clopas (John 19:25), and Mary Magdalene. The last four names are given in various Gospel stories of the crucifixion. Only three other women in Jesus' circle are named: Joanna, Suzanna, and Salome. The mother of the sons of Zebedee (in the Gospel of Matthew) may be another Mary. Later Christian legends add Mary Jacobus and Mary Salome. This excess of Marys was made more confusing by the increased popularity of the Virgin Mary and the tendency of church tradition to link all positive female roles and attributes to her. It is no surprise that another Mary, the Magdalene, would come to represent the Virgin's opposite—everything in women that is threatening and in need of control.

But the Magdalene-as-whore conflation also happened by merging the figure named Mary Magdalene (in Luke 8:2, in all four crucifixion and empty-tomb scenes, and in the resurrection stories in Matthew, John, Mark) with seven other Gospel stories that are not about her. Because she goes to the tomb of Jesus in order to anoint his body, Mary is linked to three other stories about women anointing Jesus: (1) Jesus' head is anointed by an unnamed woman in Mark 14:3–9 (see also Matthew 26:6–13); this is a prophetic gesture, interpreted by Jesus as anticipating his burial. (2) John tells the story of a woman who anointed Jesus' feet with perfume (12:1–8), again a prophetic gesture interpreted as an anointing for burial. The anointing woman is named Mary, the sister of Lazarus and Martha of Bethany in John 11:1. (3) Most important is Luke's account of an unnamed "woman in the city, who was a sinner" who wets Jesus' feet with her tears, wipes them with her hair, kisses his feet, and anoints them with ointment from an alabaster jar. She is forgiven by Jesus because she had loved much (7:36–50).

These anointing stories read like three versions of one ancient story of a woman prophet anointing Jesus as Messiah. It may already be depoliticized by Mark's emphasis on burial, and it may have been radically rewritten by Luke who turns the anointing prophet into a woman most readers have seen as a prostitute, forgiven because of her great love. I say that Luke rewrites Mark because I accept the widely held scholarly theory (called the two-source hypothesis) that Mark is the earliest Gospel (65–70 CE), and is used by Matthew and Luke when writing their Gospels in the 80s. Both Mark's and Matthew's versions show Jesus honoring the woman's prophetic role. He says, "Wherever the good news is proclaimed in the whole world, what she [the prophet] has done will be told in remembrance of her." It is possible that Luke has a separate story of an anointing woman, however his omission of Mark's story or his conflation of it with another story effectively morphs the prophet into the whore. No longer confirming the prophetic dimension of the anointing, this moment of forgiveness for sexual sin all but obliterates the political anointing of Jesus as the Messiah (or the Christ, in Greek). The prophetic act becomes a gesture of hospitality, gratitude, lavish sensuality, and love. In fact, the anointing itself is not central in Luke's version. Rather, the focus shifts to the emotional extravagance of the woman's actions, to Jesus' acceptance of such a person, and to his forgiving her. Conflated with the Mary Magdalene texts, Luke's scene of an unnamed, sinful woman becomes the centerpiece of the later Magdalene legends.

Joined also to the Magdalene legend at times were four other stories: (4) Mary of Bethany who sits at Jesus' feet while her sister Martha waits on him (Luke 10:38–42); (5) the woman taken in adultery (John 7:53–8:11); (6) the Samaritan woman (John 4:4–42), these latter two often mistaken for prostitutes; and (7) the anonymous bride of the wedding feast at Cana (John 2:1–11). It is not difficult to understand why this happened. There are lots of smaller links between the seven stories: Simon (1, 3), Bethany (1, 2), sexual "sin" (3, 5, 6), a rebuke addressed to a woman, and her defense by Jesus (1, 2, 3, 5, 6), and a woman at Jesus' feet (2, 3, 4). A woman's tears (3) and anointing for burial (1, 2) are easily linked to Mary Magdalene at the cross and weeping at the tomb. A woman's touch is mentioned (3) when Simon muses that if Jesus were a prophet, "he would have known who and what kind of woman this is who is touching him—that she is a sinner" (Luke 7:39). In John 20:17, the risen Jesus says to Mary Magdalene, "Do not touch me [or: hold on to me]." A woman's love is praised (3), and although love is not mentioned in the other texts, it may be the dominant feeling readers associate with the women who stand by Jesus at the cross and who visit his tomb.

Sometimes interested readers create the conflation. When we see the echoes and allusions in these texts, we create the connections ourselves. Silences in narratives are gaps in which the readers question, link texts, and create. The process of such conflating and legend-making yields not three but *one* anointing of Jesus: by Mary Magdalene, "the sinner," whose act is penitential and loving, not prophetic. The scholar, in contrast, may say that historically speaking only one anointing occurred during the ministry of Jesus, a prophetic action by an unnamed woman. As is common in an oral culture, this anointing most likely proliferated into three literary versions, none of which concerned Mary Magdalene. Her only connection with anointing is that she went to anoint the body of Jesus, but found the tomb empty (Mark 14:1 and Luke 24:1).

Sometimes readers want a more complete story of the life of Mary Magdalene. Through conflation one can get a richer biography of this woman who—like the unnamed woman prophet—was clearly more important to the story of Jesus than the Gospel writers tell us. Someone who is crucial to the ending of a story cannot—should not—come out of nowhere (as she does in Mark, Matthew, and John; and almost in Luke except for 8:1–3). All these motives behind the conflation may be regarded as benign, even creative.

However, the creation of this biography gave the Magdalene a past of sexual sinfulness that could be exploited and expanded. Even initially, there is much more to this process than just confusion or benign creativity. It was Luke, in my opinion, who downgraded the anointing woman in Mark 14 from prophet to "sinner," implying that her sin was sexual promiscuity, or prostitution. In the tradition, Luke 7 has overpowered and overwritten the story in Mark 14 about the prophet. Luke also puts the story of the "sinner" right next to the first mention of Mary Magdalene in 8:2. This process of confla-tion also covers up the power and authority of a woman prophet and a major witness to the resurrection. Unless we hold that the anoint-ing prophet actually *was* Mary Magdalene—and I am not sure how that possibility can be supported—it appears that the Magdalene inherited the slur Luke directed against the unnamed prophet. Backlash against the Magdalene builds on backlash against the woman prophet.

Women Speaking Nonsense

There is one more important factor in the production of Mary's legend. Luke and Mark link Mary Magdalene to demonic posses-sion. Luke says that seven demons had come out of her (8:2); one version of Mark says that Jesus cast them out (16:9). Here is a great imaginative opportunity for the legend makers: what kind of demons would a woman have? Sexual, of course. And seven, indicat-ing intensity, totality. This monstrous demonic possession is usually presented in film and video as senseless sounds, garbled or improper speech, a roaring that must be silenced.

In the ancient world, many people thought women were more susceptible than men to being invaded by spirits—good or bad ones—because a female body has more openings than a male's. This means that the legitimacy of women's prophecy—being filled with a spirit and speaking—is connected to the sexual purity or impurity of women prophets. The Apostle Paul makes this connection when he discusses women's speaking as well as women's veiling and mar-riage in his first letter to the Corinthians. In both the Hebrew Bible* and the Christian Testament, the pattern is a common one: the powerful woman is disempowered and remembered as a whore or whorish. It happens to the stories of Elijah's opponent Jezebel (1

Kings 18, 19, 21; 2 Kings 9) with her painted eyes and adorned head (2 Kings 9:30), the Samaritan woman and her multiple relationships (John 4), and the prophet of Thyatira, "that woman Jezebel, who calls herself a prophet . . . [and] refuses to repent of her fornication" (Rev 2:20–23). Both Mary Magdalene and Moses' sister Miriam (Numbers 12) are demoted from prominence to repentance. Having illegitimate religious views is often linked to sexual impurity. When the prophets criticize Israel for turning from God, they call the nation a whore and an adulteress.

The writer of Luke may have made a connection between female prophecy and spirit possession when he wrote the book of Acts. In Acts 16:16–19 we find a curious story of a slave girl, said to be "possessed with a spirit of divination." She brought her masters much profit by "fortune-telling." In the city of Philippi she followed Paul and Silas, yelling, "These men are the servants of the Most High God, who proclaim to you the way of salvation." Paul is annoyed by this—we do not know why—and one day commands the spirit to come out of her. The exorcism works and the slave girl's masters are so distressed at their loss of profit from the girl that they bring Paul and Silas before the authorities. Luke passes on without comment on the accuracy of the girl's message or her fate after she has lost her power. In this way both Paul and the author effectively silence the girl.

This all suggests to me that the claim that Mary Magdalene was demon-possessed may not be based on historical memory. It may be, rather, a trace of early efforts to undermine her authority. Perhaps what a woman thinks and what she has to say can be every bit as alarming as what she does with her body. Focusing mostly on her body may be a way of decapitating her, removing her mind, identity, voice. Whether Luke created her seven demons or not, Mary's madness could stand for resistance and subversion. It could represent rage and brave protest against kyriarchy,* that is, a kind of sanity. In this sense, her madness would be a preferable alternative to healing, unless with the healing came further power and speech, not taming and submission. As it stands, however, in Luke 8:1–3, Mary Magdalene's demon-possession is in her past. She appears with "certain women who had been healed of evil spirits and infirmities." The implication is clear that she and they follow Jesus out of gratitude (no such motivation is suggested for the male disciples). The women are silent, serving Jesus and the Twelve. They will be accused later of speaking nonsense about an empty tomb (Luke 24:11). They are indirectly vindicated only when the male disciples, particularly Simon Peter, claim that they have seen Jesus (Luke 24:33–48).

From Luke to Legend

We do not really know exactly how Mary Magdalene's story developed into the elaborate and entertaining medieval legends about her early prostitution and her saintly life of repentance in France. As early as the second century, she and Mary of Bethany (Martha and Lazarus's sister) are considered by some to be the same person.[3] Tertullian, Irenaeus, Hippolytus, and Origen are the only major writers of the second and third centuries to deal with Mary Magdalene.

Around 248 CE, Origen wrote *Against Celsus* to refute the writings of a non-Christian philosopher. Apparently, the Gospel stories about Mary Magdalene at the empty tomb were known among non-Christians since Celsus interprets them negatively, and uses them to criticize the Christian belief in resurrection:

> But we must examine this question whether anyone who really died ever rose again with the same body. Or do you think that . . . the

ending of your tragedy is to be regarded as noble and convincing—
his cry from the cross when he expired, and the earthquake and the
darkness? While he was alive he did not help himself, but after death
he rose again and showed the marks of his punishment and how his
hands had been pierced. But who saw this? A *hysterical female*, as you
say, and perhaps some other one of those who were deluded by the
same sorcery, who either dreamt in a certain state of mind and
through wishful thinking had a hallucination due to some mistaken
notion (an experience which has happened to thousands), or, which
is more likely, wanted to impress others by telling this fantastic tale,
and so by this cock-and-bull story to provide a chance for other
beggars.[4]

The reference to "other beggars" connects the "hysterical female"
at the tomb with Celsus's view of the disreputable lifestyle of this
movement in general. Origen counters the accusation of "beggary"
by alluding to Luke 8:1–3: "For in the Gospels certain women who
had been healed from their ailments, among whom was Suzanna,
provided the disciples with meals out of their own substance. But
what philosopher who was devoted to the benefit of his pupils did
not receive from them money for his needs? Or was it proper and
right for them to do this, whereas when Jesus' disciples do it, they
are accused by Celsus of collecting their means of livelihood in a
disgraceful and importunate way?"[5] Origen's reply suggests that Celsus criticized Christians by insinuating that Jesus took more than
money from his women followers or that he lived off of their prostitution. Perhaps in the second century the Magdalene was tarred
with the same accusation of disreputability directed against all of
Jesus' women associates.

Other texts from the early church show the beginnings of the
conflation of the Magdalene and the "sinful" woman of Luke 7.
Most interesting is Tertullian (ca. 160–225), who says that the

touch of "the woman which was a sinner" proved that Jesus was "not an empty phantom but a really solid body."[6] Elsewhere, referring to the scene in which the Magdalene sees the risen Jesus in the garden (John 20:11–18), Tertullian speaks of the faithful woman who approached Jesus to touch him "out of love," not out of curiosity nor unbelief.[7] There is no mention of love in John 20, but love is the trademark of the "sinner" in Luke 7. Although Tertullian shows us the link being made between the Magdalene and the "sinful" woman, he is not really interested in Mary, but rather in the theological debates of his time about whether Jesus' physical body was resurrected or just his spirit. We see the same use of Mary's touch in John 20:17 by Irenaeus (ca. 130–200) when he argues that Jesus' risen body had substance.[8]

A sermon once attributed to Hippolytus (ca. 170–235) makes different connections for the Magdalene—to Mary of Bethany, to the sensuous lover of the Song of Songs, and to the original temptress of biblical tradition, Eve. The sermon depicts Martha and Mary seeking Christ in the garden (as Mary Magdalene does in John 20). The women represent the woman in the Song of Songs who searches for her lover and finds him. In these women, the sin of the first Eve is corrected by their obedience. "Eve has become apostle." The women are "apostles to the apostles" sent not only by angels but by Christ himself, who then appears to the males to confirm the women's message.[9]

In the fourth century, there is more discussion of Mary Magdalene, with over thirty references to her by Ambrose, Jerome, the Cappadocians, Chrysostom, Augustine, and others, almost all direct references to John 20:17 and the ongoing discussion about the nature of the resurrected body of Jesus (Was he truly a man? Did he rise physically from the dead?). In the fourth-century texts we begin to see two developments that will be important for the full-blown

Magdalene legends: (1) criticism of the Magdalene's faith and intelligence. For example, Jerome says that because she did not believe Jesus had risen and thought him to be still in the tomb, she was not worthy to touch him;[10] and (2) the further merging of her image and role with that of Eve. The second is a way of accepting her status as messenger from the risen Jesus. It is an appropriate redemption of the offense of woman in general, as it was a woman who first brought the message of sin.[11] In a saying of Gregory of Nyssa (ca. 330–395), the Magdalene is Eve: "She is the first witness of the resurrection, that she might set straight again by her faith in the resurrection, what was turned over by her transgression."[12] Like the story of Eve, Mary Magdalene's story is becoming the story of all women.

One should not forget, however, that these writings come from the same time as the gnostic documents (discussed in the next chapter). The church "fathers" apparently did not directly or explicitly attack contemporary gnostic views of the Magdalene as a leader of primary importance and insight. Celsus mentions those "who follow Mariamme" as well as other leaders, but Origen dismisses this with a wave of his hand—"he pours on us a heap of names."[13] Perhaps these are the most effective methods of response: silence, conflation, focus on other issues, other personalities, other texts. In this way, Mary Magdalene is quietly reduced and demeaned.

Things get noisier in the sixth century when stories of penitent whores become popular in European Christianity. This is obvious in a sermon from Pope Gregory the Great (ca. 540–604). Here is the conflation in all its glory when Mary Magdalene, the "sinner" of Luke 7, and Mary of Bethany are presented as the same woman:

> She whom Luke calls the sinful woman, whom John calls Mary, we
> believe to be the Mary from whom seven devils were ejected according
> to Mark. And what did these seven devils signify, if not all the

vices. . . . It is clear, brothers, that the woman previously used the unguent to perfume her flesh in forbidden acts. What she therefore displayed more scandalously, she was now offering to God in a more praiseworthy manner. She had coveted with earthly eyes, but now through penitence these are consumed with tears. She displayed her hair to set off her face, but now her hair dries her tears. She had spoken proud things with her mouth, but in kissing the Lord's feet, she now planted her mouth on the Redeemer's feet. For every de-light, therefore, she had had in herself, she now immolated herself. She turned the mass of her crimes to virtues, in order to serve God entirely in penance, for as much as she had wrongly held God in contempt.[14]

Note that the demonic and the erotic are emphasized and linked. Submission is the solution. The parts of Mary's body misused in lust—her flesh, her eyes, her hair—are now properly used for adora-tion of the Lord. Her mouth, once speaking proud things, now prop-erly kisses his feet. Her entire self, once used for her own pleasure, is now properly "immolated." Gregory does two things here, really. He gives his Christian brothers an opportunity to reflect on their sins and to repent like Mary. But by choosing a female saint rather than a male one—like Peter—he also cements their views of wom-en's bodies as sexual and as highly susceptible to sexual sin and the demonic. From here, the Magdalene's legend blossoms and becomes as much about shaping medieval male monastic spirituality and worldviews as about commenting on women's sexuality, sinfulness, and redemption.

Only the Penitent Man Shall Pass

We have now arrived at the fully developed and most entertaining Mary legends. These tales are a madcap combination of stories about Mary's early life, her later life as a hermit (conflating her story with yet another Mary—the desert hermit Mary of Egypt), and her preaching the Gospel to pagans in Gaul. The earliest complete story appears in a tenth- or eleventh-century sermon once attributed to Odo of Cluny.[15] Eventually, we get the thirteenth-century Golden Legend in which, it seems, her story is completely unrelated to her portrayal in the Bible.

Different writers created different emphases within the same basic story, depending on whether their interest was in the roles of women, disputes over church privilege and wealth, the mystery of grace, the nature of the contemplative life, individual spirituality, or a conflict between conservatives and reformers. The stress on her role as a preacher in Gaul can be traced to Rabanus Maurus (ca. 844), who said that by her preaching she had filled the universe with the scent of the news of Christ. He is nicely conflating her with Mary of Bethany who anointed Jesus in John 12:3 ("The house was filled with the fragrance of the perfume"). In the twelfth century, Abbot Hugh of Semur (d. 1109), Peter Abelard (d. 1142), Geoffrey of Vendome (d. 1132), and others referred to Mary Magdalene as the sinner who merited the title "apostle to the apostles." The title appears frequently in twelfth- and thirteenth-century stories, scripture interpretation, hymns, and art. At this time, the Magdalene could be talked about openly as an apostle. Apparently, Luke's "sinner" had been so successfully conflated with her that her saintliness and her apostolic status were not threatening. Perhaps the counterweight of her sinfulness had made it safe to speak of her power and authority.

By and large, only the Western church conflated various Marys and unnamed women with Mary Magdalene. The Eastern church has always held that Mary Magdalene, Mary of Bethany, and the "sinner" are different women. The legends also differ according to whether they locate Mary's last days in Palestine, Ephesus, Les Saintes-Maries-de-la-Mer in the Camargue in southeastern France, or Aix or Marseilles in Provence, also in France. The East preferred the Ephesian legend, which plays on the tradition that Mary Magdalene was engaged to John the Evangelist, who abandoned her when he was called away from their wedding at Cana to be a disciple of Christ. Honorius of Autun (early twelfth century) summarizes: "She fled to Jerusalem, where, unmindful of her birth, forgetful of the law of God, she became a common prostitute and of her own free will set up a brothel of sin and made it in truth a temple of demons, for seven devils entered into her and plagued her continually with foul desires."[16] Marguerite Yourcenar makes use of this story in her novel *Fires* (1981), spicing it up in the Western fashion. John's abandonment causes Mary's prostitution and an unsuccessful attempt to seduce Jesus at Simon's house. She becomes a disciple who rivals John. At the empty tomb she muses: "For the second time in my life, I was standing in front of a deserted bed."

In the Eastern church, after Jesus ascends to the heavens, Mary follows John to Ephesus. The legend says that she died there and was buried in the cave of the Seven Sleepers. According to this legend, her relics and those of John were later taken to the church of St. Lazarus in Constantinople by Emperor Leo VI.

The Western tradition is a vibrant collage of adventure, miracles, and visions. The most complete version of the Provençal legend dates from around 1267 and is called "The Golden Legend." It was written down by Jacobus de Voragine (d. 1298), the Dominican archbishop of Genoa. It was wildly popular and so was Mary. There are over 700 manuscripts and 173 printed editions of the Golden Legend. In Western Europe, over 190 shrines were dedicated to Mary Magdalene, and more than 600 of her relics venerated. In pre-Reformation England, there were 170 churches bearing her name.

William Caxton's 1483 Golden Legend in Middle English was the last full-scale version published in English before the Reformation. It disappeared not because people lost interest in Mary Magdalene, but because it was "a victim of a conscious policy of the Protestant state, bent on obliterating all material associated with Catholicism."[17]

Since the Golden Legend is the primary medieval Magdalene legend, let me summarize it here.[18] Mary Magdalene, her sister Martha, and her brother Lazarus were born of royal, wealthy parents. So entirely had Mary "abandoned her body to pleasure that she was no longer called by any other name than 'the sinner.'" One day, by divine inspiration, she entered the house of Simon the leper, the Pharisee of Bethany, where the Lord was at dinner. She bathed his feet with her tears of penance, dried them with her hair, anointed them with precious ointment. Although the Pharisee objected, the Lord forgave her.

"And thenceforth there was no grace that He refused her, nor any mark of affection that He withheld from her" (there is no indication as far as I can see that this is meant erotically). He delivered her from seven devils, "admitted her to His friendship, condescended to dwell in her house, and was pleased to defend her whenever the occasion arose" (before the Pharisee, Martha, and Judas). He raised Lazarus from the dead "for love of her" whom he could not see in tears without himself weeping. "Magdalene also had the honour of being present at the death of Jesus, standing at the foot of the Cross; and it was she that anointed His body with sweet spices after His death, and who stayed at the sepulchre when all the disciples went away. And to her first the risen Jesus appeared and made her apostle to the apostles."

Thus the great bulk of the beginning of the story rests on conflated Christian Testament texts. Afterward there is no more attention paid to the passion and resurrection scenes. The notion of her great wealth is not connected to financial support of Jesus and the Twelve, but rather serves to emphasize her prior life of luxury. The figures with which the Magdalene was conflated have overwhelmed her. Emphasis is on her sin and repentance, and on love.

The story continues fourteen years after Jesus' Ascension. When the disciples went out to preach, St. Peter entrusted Mary Magdalene to St. Maximinus. With Lazarus, Martha, Martilla (Martha's servant), Maximinus, and other Christians, Mary Magdalene was put out to sea by "the infidels" (that is, the Jews) in a boat without a rudder, in the hope that all would drown. But they landed safely at Marseilles and were sheltered under the portico of a pagan temple. When Mary Magdalene saw the pagans going into their temple to offer sacrifice to their gods, she began to preach Christ to them. "And all wondered at her, not only for her beauty, but for her eloquence, which eloquence was not indeed a matter of surprise on lips that had touched the Lord's feet." She converted the prince and princess of Marseilles and successfully threatened them with punishment for their neglect of the poor "servants of God."

One day when the Magdalene was preaching, the ruler asked if she could give proof of the faith she preached. She answered that her preaching was confirmed by miracles "and through the preaching of Peter, my master, the bishop of Rome!" Even though she interceded with God to obtain the conception of a child for him, the prince wished to consult St. Peter "in order to know whether all that Magdalene said of Christ were true." On the journey to Rome, during a storm at sea, the princess gave birth prematurely and died. Her body and the living newborn infant were abandoned on a hilly coast. Blaming Mary Magdalene, but commending his wife and child to her and to God, the prince continued on to Rome and was received there by St. Peter, who accompanied him on a pilgrimage to Jerusalem. After two years' instruction in the faith by

Peter, the prince started back to Marseilles. Along the way, the child ("whom Mary Magdalene had taken into her care, watching over him from afar to keep him alive") was found. As the prince offered a short prayer to Mary Magdalene, the body of the princess came alive. She announced that "when Saint Peter led thee about Jerusalem, showing thee scenes of Christ's life and death, I too was there, with Mary Magdalene as my guide."

Finally back in Marseilles, the royal couple was baptized by Maximinus, and the citizens of Marseilles replaced all pagan temples with Christian churches. Lazarus was chosen to be bishop of Marseilles, and when Mary and her followers went to Aix, Maximinus was elected bishop there. This portion of the legend is interesting for its subordination of Mary Magdalene to Peter, its attribution to her of fertility powers, and its emphasis on her preaching.

The last phase of the story concerns the retirement of Mary Magdalene to a mountain cave, where she spent her last thirty years in contemplative isolation, without friends and family, without even ravens to feed her like Elijah. Her lack of "earthly satisfaction" there is not explicitly explained as punishment or penance, though shortly before her death she introduces herself to a priest in the wilderness in this way: "Dost thou recall having read in the Gospel the story of Mary, the notorious sinner who washed the Savior's feet, wiped them with the hairs of her head, and obtained pardon for all her sins? . . . I am that sinner." She sent the priest to Maximinus to tell him to expect her to appear to him on the day after Easter. When she appeared, raised above the earth and surrounded by angels, her face was radiant. After she received her last Eucharist, "her body fell lifeless before the altar and her soul took its flight to the Lord." Maximinus buried her and commanded that he be buried beside her at his death. The legend ends with an alternate, less dramatic death account, an account of the theft of her relics from Aix to Vézelay, the author's insistence that the story of Mary's betrothal to John is "a false and frivolous tale," and five stories of her post-burial miracles.

All that material at the end shows that Mary's legend was under construction and dispute. For the writer, the Eastern church's legend of Mary's connection to John must be refuted. The contest between Aix and Vézelay for the most authentic claim to Mary's relics must be settled. The monastery at Vézelay in Burgundy was making the loudest claim to possess Mary's bones, becoming for a time the site of the most celebrated and economically productive pilgrimage in France. Some identified Mary's cave with the grotto of Ste. Baume (Holy Balm), high up in the mountains of Provence, east of Marseilles, near the town of St. Maximin. A flood of saint materials evolving over two hundred years developed different versions of how she got from Palestine to France and with whom, and how her bones got from Marseilles to Vézelay. In the thirteenth century, Vézelay was upstaged by St. Maximin's claim to possess the body, and the pilgrims started coming to Provence, as they still do today, to see her skull paraded about encased in gold during her feast days in July.

Later in the fifteenth century, the bodies of her companions were said to have been discovered at a town at the mouth of the Rhone, Notre Dame de la Mer, renamed Les Stes Maries de-la-Mer. The shrine there is dedicated to Mary Salome, Mary Jacobe, and Mary Magdalene. Even today the Marys are celebrated there in May, with their companion or servant black Sara, patron saint of the Roma (gypsies). On feast days the dressed-up statues are carried back to the Mediterranean, their escort mounted on the white Camargue horses, thousands of onlookers lining the beach.

The Christian Testament Magdalene has all but disappeared by the dramatic conclusion of the Golden Legend, which developed in the context of ecclesiastical financial dealings, monastic rivalries, the cult of relics, the politics of pilgrimage, and ideals of feminine asceticism.* But this is not the only spin on the Magdalene in this period. A bit earlier than the Golden Legend is the little known *The Life of St. Mary Magdalene*,[19] influenced by the spiritual, mystical doctrine of Bernard of Clairvaux. Like the more popular Golden Legend, this work conflates Christian Testament texts. But its tone and emphases are quite different.

This legend focuses on the Christian Testament profile of the Magdalene rather than her post-ascension career in France. The stories of her naked solitude in the cave and angelic transport are dismissed as false, and nothing is said about a rudderless boat or the prince and princess of Marseilles. Like the Golden Legend, Mary's early life of sexual sin results from her youth, physical attractiveness, "the weakness of the [female] sex," and wealth. There is an extended contrast between Mary and Eve (chap. 27). Her role as a traveler with Jesus in his career is acknowledged, but she is later said to stay behind at home often with her sister Martha, sending supplies to Jesus and his followers (chaps. 9, 11).

The story celebrates her friendship and intimacy with Christ, their "mutual love" (chap. 15), and his humanity. She is his "first servant" (chaps. 24, 26), "special friend," and "the most tenderly loved among all women except for the Virgin Mother of God" (chap. 27). This love is presented erotically, emphasizing the caressing massage of his feet and hair (chaps. 17–18), her grief like that of a forsaken lover (chap. 33), his "sweet embraces," and her being like a bride (chap. 45). But their relationship is also chaste (chap. 8). The story uses a lot of sexual imagery but Mary never becomes an actual lover or mother: "Impregnated [by Jesus] with [the seven gifts of the] Spirit, by faith she conceived a good hope within herself, and gave birth to a fervent charity" (chap. 6).

Mary Magdalene is depicted as eyewitness to all the events of the passion of Jesus (chaps. 20–23); she is, however, excluded from the last supper. "Loyalty did not forsake Mary Magdalene. The skin of her flesh adhered to the bones of the Saviour, for when Judas betrayed him, Peter denied him, and the ten apostles fled from him, there was still found in Mary Magdalene the courage of the Redeemer" (chap. 20). Her loyalty illustrates that "love is as strong as death" (chap. 21). Almost identified with Christ on the cross ("Christ was pierced with nails on the cross; the soul of Mary was pierced with sharp grief," chap. 21), she is once said to be a "man" ("a man's soul was manifested in a woman") because she fulfills a passage attributed to Solomon ("My hands dripped with myrrh," chap. 23).

It is not Peter, but Mary Magdalene who is the first to see the risen Lord. She, not the Beloved Disciple, is the first to believe. And she is the first to announce the resurrection and predict the ascension (chaps. 25–27, 29). All this makes her an apostle, evangelist, and prophet, and, because of her conversion and intimacy with Christ, more than a prophet (chaps. 29, 32).

But she is not primarily a preacher. She becomes a maid to the Virgin Mary, and her companion in contemplation (chaps. 34–35). Peter, who sets up his "patriarchal throne" in Antioch, delegates the Western regions to male preachers, and Maximinus is sent to Gaul. Mary Magdalene joins and entrusts herself to him (chaps. 36–37). While Maximinus preaches and new faith springs up, Mary devotes herself primarily to contemplation ("for she was in fact the most ardent lover of the Redeemer, the woman who had wisely chosen the best part which—witness God—was never taken from her once she received it from Christ at his feet"). But "also mindful of the well-being of her friends," she "from time to time" leaves the joys of contemplation and preaches to the unbelievers and believers, presenting herself to sinners as an example of conversion, and becoming "an evangelist for believers throughout the world" (chap. 38).

On the whole, it is difficult to say which the author has empha-sized more, her sin/conversion/penitence or her role as witness/apos-tle/prophet. In the post-ascension section, Mary-the-penitent-contemplative receives the heavier weight. In chapter 30 the author writes, "most happy by far [is] the one who has been so moved by and who has taken such delight in the surpassing fragrance of Mary's deeds that he has followed the example of her conversion, has imprinted in himself the image of her repentance, and has filled his spirit with her devotion, to the degree that he has made himself a partaker of that best part which she chose." Again, the women from the other stories have overwhelmed the Christian Testament Mary Magdalene. In this case, the power to tame her comes most strongly from the story of Mary of Bethany, listening and silent at the feet of Jesus. It comes from the story that many have thought of as promoting the liberation of women, but which feminist biblical scholar Elisabeth Schüssler Fiorenza has shown promotes with dan-gerous subtlety the patriarchal separation and restriction of women.[20]

In a final irony, Magdalene is finally removed from all women. When Maximinus was laid beside her, the place became "so holy that no king, prince, or other person, no matter what earthly pomp attended him, would enter the church to pray for help without mak-ing some sign of humble devotion, first disposing of his weapons and all other marks of brutal ferocity. No woman was ever so audacious as to enter that temple, no matter what condition, order, or dignity she enjoyed" (chap. 50). Perhaps the male contemplative monk has been the reader all along, his soul is a "she" urged to strive to imi-tate the Magdalene.

By the thirteenth century, Mary Magdalene had become a dis-tinctive character apart from her scriptural origins. Her story illus-trated the church's emphasis on sin, repentance, and individual responsibility. She became a model for all, for taking the sacraments

of penance and the Eucharist. She was regarded as the great excep-
tion to the Christian Testament prohibition against women preaching (1 Timothy 2). Her life of sin and penance allowed her to be
honored and extolled in the late thirteenth, fourteenth, and fifteenth centuries as an apostle without fear that she would become
a model for women in this regard. Like the Virgin Mary, she was
"alone of all her sex." After the Reformation, in Protestant and
many Catholic writings, talk of her apostleship disappeared. She
was no longer typically associated with preaching or evangelism, but
became almost exclusively a figure of penitence for Protestants, and
of penitence and contemplation for Catholics.

What can be said that is not utterly obvious about the sexual
politics of these two medieval versions of her legend? Although one
cannot know how everyday people interpreted these legends, the
conflations and additions successfully reduce the significance of the
Christian Testament Magdalene to a focus on penitence and contemplation. Forgiven, she chooses the better part, as she formerly
chose whoring. When Jesus is killed, her love will not give up on
him; he returns to her; he leaves again. She lives on as a contemplative, and/or as a naked, isolated penitent, weeping. The guilt never
really goes away. Her love becomes spiritual. In the Golden Legend,
she has miraculous power to aid others in conception, and in this
sense is finally a "mother."

Mary's medieval legends appear to give much but really give little. When the Magdalene does preach in the south of France, she
offers no real challenge to the hierarchy of the church. Authorized
by the risen Christ, she strangely has no authority. Even though she
has extravagant love for Christ, there is a controlled calmness and
prudence about her in these legends. She is a woman of warm emotion and loyalty, but not of ideas or great intelligence. She is presented as understanding herself as a sinner who has been given

mercy, and in the end she has nothing much to say to others except to point to herself as a sinner. Weeping replaces speaking. For medieval men, there is a reassurance here: you have nothing to fear from such a strong woman. For medieval women, there is a message of salvation (from female sexuality) and protection (by the male Jesus and church authorities). This is the destiny of even the greatest women. In fact this is their greatness. The power of Mary's story is primarily the power of God to redeem. When this great sinner is reconciled to God, we know that no one is beyond the reach of God's mercy.

The tenacity and force with which the Western imagination has clung to the portrait of the harlot-saint is shown in modern media presentations and in the richness of artistic portraits of the Magdalene of legend. But it can also be seen in reactions against early attempts to correct her story. In 1517, the year Luther nailed up his theses in Wittenberg, the leading French Christian humanist Dominican Jacques Lefèvre d'Etaples published a critique of the then-traditional Magdalene. Within three years, fifteen major treatises had been written on the controversy and Lefèvre had been accused of heresy, censured by the theological faculty of the Sorbonne, and his works placed on the Index of Forbidden Books. The issue was raised fiercely again in the seventeenth century, and serious debate continued until after the end of the nineteenth century. It was not simply a scholarly debate. In the mid-nineteenth-century upper- and middle-class Evangelical women working with prostitutes refuted the traditional view of Mary Magdalene, emphasizing her as the woman at the cross.[21]

Today, both Roman Catholicism and Protestantism officially agree with Eastern Orthodoxy in distinguishing among Mary Magdalene, Mary of Bethany, and the "sinner" of Luke. But it was not until 1969 that changes were made in the Roman Catholic Calendar, and not until 1978 were deletions made in the Roman Breviary (of saint's lives) wiping out her sinful reputation. Although she was reinstated as one of many followers of Jesus, her role of apostle to the apostles and preacher was erased, and her feastday reduced from "one of the most elaborate of all liturgies reserved for the most important saints," to a "memorial, a simple remembrance."[22]

Even biblical scholars talk as if the distortions have been completely reversed and everyone now knows that Mary was not a whore. John Meier comments: "it goes without saying—or should—that Mary Magdalene is not to be equated with either the 'sinful woman' of Luke 7:36–50 or the Mary of Bethany from the Johannine tradition (John 11–12). This is a commonplace in exegesis today. .... Indeed, even in 20th-century Catholic exegesis this view is nothing new."[23] It goes without saying—or should—but doesn't.

Sex and Marriage

Not only is Mary still commonly thought of as a whore, but the interest in her sexuality is alive and well. In fact, the idea that Mary and Jesus had a sexual relationship has been around for quite a while. The Catharists or Albigensians (twelfth and thirteenth centuries) held that she was Jesus' concubine. Martin Luther (early sixteenth century) assumed that they had a sexual relationship. Brigham Young (late nineteenth century) suggested in a sermon that Christ was a polygamist with Mary, Martha, and Mary Magdalene.[24] The Rosicrucians (from the seventeenth century on) suggested that Christ and Mary Magdalene had children. Erotic themes appear in some late nineteenth-century and twentieth-century art, novels, and poetry (Rodin, Rilke, D. H. Lawrence, erotic paintings of the crucifixion), and are re-visited again and again in contemporary scholarship, pseudo-scholarship, and journalistic writing.

For example, William E. Phipps's book, *Was Jesus Married?* (1970), speculates that Jesus may have married Mary Magdalene when he was in his twenties; she may have been unfaithful to him but he forgave her, an experience that influenced his views on divorce and human relationships. In *Jesus and the Riddle of the Dead Sea Scrolls* (1992), Barbara Thiering asserts from fantastic conflations and code-breaking of Christian Testament and Dead Sea Scrolls passages that Mary Magdalene was married to Jesus and they had three children. She left him and he married again. Michael Baigent, Richard Leigh, and Henry Lincoln's popular book, *Holy Blood, Holy Grail* (1983), based on investigative TV reporting and "common sense," spins a fascinating mystery about Jesus' marriage to Mary Magdalene, her arrival with their child or children in the south of France, and the finding and decoding of secret documents from the Knights Templars, the Cathars, the Rosicrucians, the Masons and others, tracing the bloodline of Jesus and the Magdalene (the Holy Grail dynasty) in the royal houses of Europe. Dan Brown's *The Da Vinci Code* builds on this book and presents—in thriller fashion—the idea that Mary is Jesus' wife and the Holy Grail itself, a vessel that bears Jesus' children.

There are still scholarly treatments of Mary Magdalene that conflate the texts too, though modern motivations differ from those of the past. Bishop John Shelby Spong suggests that the Gospels contain hints that she was linked with Jesus "in a romantic way." The marriage at Cana becomes the wedding of Jesus and Mary Magdalene, whom Spong identifies with Mary of Bethany, the anointing woman in Mark 14, and the "sinner" of Luke 7. Spong asks, "Why is there still a continuing sense, ranging from dis-ease to revulsion, that arises in us when we hear the suggestion that Jesus might have been married? I suggest that far more than any of us realize we are subconsciously victimized by the historic negativity toward women that has been a major gift of the Christian church to the world. So pervasive is this negativity that unconsciously we still regard holy matrimony to be less than the ideal, and we still operate out of an understanding of women that defines them as the source of sin, the polluter of otherwise moral men."[25]

Despite the well-meaning gender politics of both Dan Brown and Bishop Spong, making Mary Magdalene into Jesus' wife or lover seems to me just another attempt to complete the process of her "redemption" from a whore to a "normal" (married) woman. It does affirm marriage and heterosexual female sexuality, true, and this is why it appeals to some women. But primarily it is about Jesus. It serves to make him human and a "real man," with satisfied sexual urges, the ability to love fully. The Magdalene is used in a variety of ways in different periods in order to think about Jesus, and about men in general. I see her as one of Virginia Woolf's looking-glasses "possessing the magic and delicious power of reflecting the figure of man at twice its natural size."[26]

I agree with some feminist biblical scholars who suggest that we should think about Jesus, and maleness, and gender in different ways. For Elisabeth Schüssler Fiorenza, Jesus in the Christian Testament is a representation of a marginalized man who in his career and execution struggles against oppression "at the bottom of the kyriarchal pyramid."[27] Thus he is not a "real man," rather he represents Sophia-God* as a wo/man, a term that includes marginalized men. In the Gospels, Jesus disrupts the boundaries between male and female: he nurtures, is concerned for children, he wishes to comfort and stop the violence. He feeds, washes feet, he weeps, he experiences intimacy. Jesus does not need Mary Magdalene to make him a real man because he disrupts our understanding of what a "real man" is.

The Loyal, Angry Prostitute

The legends of Mary Magdalene are deeply ambiguous. Her courage and loyalty are stressed at the crucifixion and tomb, but almost always explained away as expressing only romantic love and gratitude. In some versions, she preaches and teaches; but what she says—if anything is given for her to say—simply repeats what men say. She becomes represented by and represents prostitutes; but both she and they are degraded and blamed. In the Magdalene legends a woman without children, marriage, and family is celebrated; but she winds up dramatically alone, punished forever for her autonomy. She is contemplative and spiritually talented; but the price for this is removal from human society. Through her, female sexuality is sometimes presented as saucy, never quite tamed. But the presentation is of male views only, with the sensual and the spiritual and the intellectual split apart. Her legends fail to meld these human dimensions, because she remains punishable by the memory of that from which she was "reformed."

Still, the central aspect of the legend, the identification of the Magdalene as a whore, has untapped power. It is not only a slur to be scraped off the historical figure; it also invites pondering and reuse, especially in the light of feminist analysis of prostitution and of the various voices of prostitutes themselves as they come to political speech today. Perhaps it can be read as creating good confusion, an opportunity for subversion. When women listen to each other over great differences, and form alliances, there are new powers, new questions. Not only "What is a whore?" but also " 'What is chastity?" For Taslima Nasreen—condemned to death by Islamic fundamentalists in Bangladesh—the word whore is a "virile and fatal weapon. . . . If I evoke [it] here, it is to show [men] that we [women] know what strategies they use. And a strategy becomes ineffective when it loses all its mystery."[28] A reworked image of the Magdalene as prostitute can function as a mirror for women, and help us tell the truth about our own experiences and our bodies. It can also raise the question why any population of women should be "assigned to take all the ugliness to protect the rest of us."[29]

The continuing value of her legends and art is due as well to the depiction of an exuberant and irrepressible female sexuality, of a transcendent and spiritual dimension of the beauty of the body. She is the only official saint who represents that, however distorted. Her emotional range is enormous. "Bitter tears . . . she often sheds, but she evidently knows love and fury, spiritual transport, thoughtful concentration, great dignity, and deep anxiety." "I believe," writes Anne Hollander, "that the sinful, colorful, mythical Mary still has good work to do. . . . I wouldn't want to do without the ambivalence she represents. . . . What we get from her composite image is a more realistic picture of human female experience than was ever intended."[30]

We get a glimpse of Mary's emotional range in Franco Zeffirelli's *Jesus of Nazareth.* For his former prostitute Zeffirelli chose Anne Bancroft, who strikes me as an intelligent actress with a short fuse. Mary Magdalene's final scene begins with a knock and ends with a door banging shut. It contains the Magdalene's only self-defense—as far as I know—in the history of interpretation. She comes to the hiding disciples and they sit around her as she tells how she has seen the Lord. They are silent, then embarrassed. She turns to John as the one who will surely believe her, but he does not. Mary Magdalene and John are in a power struggle; the lighting is harsh; she is old, washed out by the light, wrinkled. He tells her she's tired. As she gives up and moves angrily toward the door, one of them mutters, "women's fantasies." Here the anger of the Bancroft Magdalene comes to a healthy head. Medusa-like, she glares with contempt on the disciples. She growls, "Was his death a fantasy? . . . Why should he not appear to me? [Then coldly] He told me to tell you, and I have done so." This is also the only instance I know of the Magdalene's anger. She flings back the bar of the door, and slams out. The door slowly springs back open. The doorway is empty.

The movie, however, is not over. It proceeds to its ending in an all-male world. First there is a discussion about who among the disciples believes and who doesn't. Eventually Peter believes. Talk turns to forgiveness, and Peter speaks of a "we" that excludes the women. He speaks of "we" who are all cowards, who all betrayed him, all abandoned him. Now "we" are all forgiven. It seems that the viewer is supposed to be drawn into that "we" by Peter's direct look at the camera. The Magdalene's message about an empty tomb is disappearing under the weight of Peter's belief. Her meaning is reduced again to forgiveness, and even that appropriated, blotted out, by the character of Peter.

Big deal. He's forgiven, we're all forgiven, and the Magdalene is gone. Her function has been to bring a message to the men who matter. She confronts, she leaves; they appropriate her belief; they go on. No one has asked her to stay; no one goes after her; her absence is not mourned; no one in the movie gives her a thought when she's gone. In the final moments of the film, Jesus comes to the disciples; they gather around him and are sent out to make disciples. "I am with you always," he says. Blah, blah, blah. For me as a viewer, the power of the Magdalene's last scene and the empty door has drained the power from these all-male scenes. It makes them look hokier than usual, even more false. It de-ends the ending. The film cannot conclude on the note it seems intended to end on, of firm resolution that would enable the spectator to put Mary out of her/his mind. In spite of Peter's attempt to pull me in, I am a resistant viewer, long gone, out the door with the Magdalene.

Where does she go? Into pre-Christian or post-Christian space? At the cross, she was with the other women. Is she alone again now, or in the potentially subversive world of female bonding? There has been a glimpse in this film of female self-empowerment—and most importantly, more than a glimpse of female anger. The powerful absence Mary leaves in the final scene lingers in my memory. Mary Magdalene has made her exodus, her escape. What is she doing out there? Mary's absence from the open, empty doorway draws our attention to the experience of many women and men with kyriarchal religions. I read the doorway as leaving open the possibility not that she will come back, but that the men can get out, that they too can exit from a tomb that is not (yet) empty.

But to where? What are we to do with the distortion, the legend? In the gnostic materials discussed in the next chapter, Mary Magdalene is not labeled whore or sinner, nor is her story confused or combined with those of other women. Instead, other traits of the Magdalene traditions are emphasized: her apostleship and speaking. The gnostic version of Mary is not perfect. It has its own frustrating compromises. But it survived in these buried texts like an underground spring. In some of the gnostic materials, the anger of the male disciples flares up. The twenty-first century reader may experience anger too, over a heritage pushed aside.

CHAPTER 3

The Woman Who Understood (Too) Completely

> Whenever you see a board up with "Trespassers will
> be prosecuted," trespass at once.
>
> VIRGINIA WOOLF
> on her father's advice to walkers

SOONER OR LATER someone will write a thrilling novel that uncovers the secret feminist cabal that forged the thirteen books found in Egypt in 1945, now called the Nag Hammadi library. After her legends, the image of Mary Magdalene as a visionary with spiritual insight, a confidant and companion of Jesus, and a leader of the disciples, seems too good to be true. These texts and others outside the Christian Testament offer feminine images of the divine, criticism of traditional Christianity, and a theological emphasis on seeking and striving rather than obedience and atoning for sins. Did someone create these texts just to influence contemporary debates about gender, sexuality, inclusive language, or even Jesus' sex life? In several of these texts, men protesting Mary Magdalene's importance and even presence seem like early, angry versions of current struggles over women's leadership in church and society.

Of course, there is also no ideal feminist Christianity to be found in these ancient texts. If we were archaeologists digging to the bedrock of the Magdalene tradition, and we found the evidence discussed in this chapter, it would not be like finding a beautiful, intact marble statue of Mary, or Sophia, or the Goddess. It would be like finding a mother lode of new shards and fragments, evidence that complicates our ideas about ancient Christianity and gives us only glimpses of a Mary we had not known before except, perhaps, by guessing or imagination. Sifting this layer of the tradition will not result in big claims about who Mary Magdalene really was. But the glimpses of Mary here disrupt the Christian Testament Mary and destabilize the claims and authority of canon and church. Perhaps that is why they were pushed outside in the first place. And maybe that is why these ancient texts appear so relevant to our struggles today, because things that interrupt and challenge the power arrangements in church and society are often, still, pushed aside.

The Problems with the Term "Gnosticism"

The Nag Hammadi library contains fifty-two religious texts— Christian, Jewish, and pagan—accidentally found by Muhammad Ali, a peasant digging for nitrates for fertilizer near the town of Nag Hammadi in Upper Egypt. Most of them contain ideas formerly known only second-hand, from the harsh criticisms and ridicule of church writers railing against their opponents. The books were hidden in a jar around 400 CE, possibly to preserve them from Roman Christian "heresy" hunters. In these texts, we can hear, at least partially, the ancient voices of some gnostics. Although there is much more work to be done studying these texts, their discovery has revolutionized our understanding of early Christianity.

Five of the Nag Hammadi texts give Mary Magdalene a prominent role, surprisingly unlike the roles she plays in the legends and in the Christian Testament. These texts are the Gospel of Thomas, the Dialogue of the Savior, the First Apocalypse of James, the Gospel of Philip, and the Sophia of Jesus Christ. Before the Nag Hammadi find, several other ancient texts had already been discovered that mention Mary Magdalene: the Pistis Sophia, the Gospel of Peter, the Gospel of Mary, Psalms of Heracleides, Epistula Apostolorum, Apostolic Church Order, and the Acts of Philip. In the first years of their discoveries, many treated these texts casually, and without a full sense of their significance for the study of women in early Christianity. Now they can be used to add to our understanding of Mary Magdalene.

These texts might appear strange to people familiar with the Christian Testament. They sound philosophical and bizarre, with their talk of the Light, and the Powers, and their puzzling abstractions. What kind of Christians interpreted Jesus in this way and produced books like these? This is a complex question that cannot be solved here. Traditionally, the texts are said to come from so-called heretical Christian groups called "Gnostics." There are problems with both terms: *heretical* and *gnostic*. These terms and others like them (*orthodox* or *marginal* or *mainline*) create the false impression that the lines between various Christian groups were clear, and that anyone could tell which groups were *truly* Christian and which were not. Actually, there never was a version of Christianity called "Gnosticism." That term was popularized by scholars in the eighteenth and nineteenth centuries to refer to all kinds of "heresies" in early Christianity. The early church writer Irenaeus (ca. 130–200) sarcastically called his opponents gnostics in order to ridicule their claims to knowledge.

There are a lot of misconceptions about "Gnostics" and "Gnosticism." If you are interested in further discussion, I encourage you to read the work of Karen King or Elaine Pagels. For now, here are some features that I associate with gnostics: (1) an emphasis on knowledge (*gnosis*, in Greek) as a means of salvation, rather than faith or obedience; (2) an emphasis on seeking the truth of one's own divine, inner self, whose true origin and home are somehow beyond the physical or worldly (that is, are transcendent); (3) an emphasis on visionary experience and mystical religious practices that give people insight into the true nature of reality.

In order to avoid giving the impression that there were real organizations or individuals who called themselves gnostic, I use the term without quotation marks and without capitalization. Even so, I use it with lots of reservations that I ask you to keep in mind: (1) gnostic texts show a lot of variety; (2) gnostics were never a clear-cut group or sect or movement or religion; (3) the relationship among the texts, grouped in this chapter because they mention Mary, is not at all clear; (4) some of the texts—for example, the Gospel of Mary or the Gospel of Thomas—are not gnostic according to anything but the widest use of the term: that is, they are gnostic only in that they seem to share an emphasis on the saving significance of experiential religious knowledge; and (5) their relationship to the Christian Testament and its traditions is at present uncertain.

Cautiously grouping these texts together provides a range of Mary Magdalene traditions very different from the ones discussed in the previous chapter, and very different from those in the Christian Testament. Investigating them is hard work because the texts are fragmentary, the terminology is unfamiliar, and the results are tentative. But the hope is that the reader will be energized by the excitement of dawning insights. In these texts one can hear gnostics and near-gnostics talking about Mary Magdalene, and giving voice to their ideas of her. These ideas can change both our view of the past and our view of the future.

An Alternative Mary Magdalene

Although the materials in which Mary Magdalene appears have distinctive and sometimes conflicting emphases, it is possible to sketch an overarching profile. Perfect precision is impossible, even with the individual works. The major texts have big holes (literally), others are only fragments, there are many serious translation difficulties, and next to nothing is really known of the social make-up of various Christian groups. Sketching a profile from these diverse texts produces a kind of counter-conflation to the Mary of Western legend. Chapter 2 shows how many stories about and not about Mary get conflated into the legend of Mary the repentant prostitute. This chapter shows that some people emphasized other aspects of Mary's story and brought together different ideas about her. Neither the Western legend nor my profile of the non-canonical* Mary can get to the historical Mary Magdalene, but knowing about both shows that people are always using Mary for their own purposes. The choices people make always make a difference.

My profile has nine points, each appearing in at least four texts: (1) Mary is prominent among the followers of Jesus; (2) she exists in a textual world of male-centered language and kyriarchal ideology; (3) she speaks boldly; (4) she is a visionary; (5) she is praised for her superior understanding; (6) she is identified as the intimate companion of Jesus; (7) she plays a leadership role in relationship to the male disciples; (8) she is opposed by or in open conflict with one or more of the male disciples; (9) she is defended. After looking at these themes in several texts, I will look at the Gospel of Mary, which features all nine aspects of the profile.

Mary's Prominence (#1) in Male-Centered Texts (#2)

In contrast to the Christian Testament texts, Mary is prominent in many of the gnostic texts. She is named among the disciples. She speaks. People speak to her. In the Gospel of Thomas, Mary is one of five disciples who speak. Mary is not depicted as a leader like James the Just (12), and does not receive special revelation like Thomas (13), but she asks Jesus questions and speaks for the entire group (21). In the Sophia of Jesus Christ (90, 17–19), Mary is the only one named of the seven women who followed the Redeemer into Galilee after he rose from the dead (also in the First Apocalypse of James). In Pistis Sophia, Mary Magdalene is the most prominent disciple of Jesus and his chief conversation partner, asking more questions than all the other disciples (67 of 115 in parts I–III). She is the first of the disciples to speak and is often their spokesperson and interpreter. Mary Magdalene is listed first among the women disciples in the Manichaean Psalm Book.

Before rushing to rescue the Mary of these texts as a feminist heroine, one must acknowledge how this prominent Mary exists in a textual world of male-centered language, theology, and ideology. It is not difficult to see the sexism in these texts ranging from ideas about men as perfect and strong and women as imperfect and weak to outright misogyny. In all of these texts, women characters are a minority, and men do most of the talking. In these texts, as in all societies, women sometimes speak in favor of their own oppression.

Androcentric* language is used to define human salvation. In the Sophia of Jesus Christ, Jesus calls the future gnostic Christians "the masculine [multitude]," and speaks of "the defect of the female."[1]

In the Gospel of Philip, only "free men and virgins" are Christians, excluding "defiled women," who have participated in "the marriage of defilement," which may refer to all sexual intercourse. When one drinks "the cup of prayer" that contains wine and water and is full of the holy spirit, one receives "the perfect man." When one goes down into the baptismal water, one puts on "the living man."[2]

There is an interesting exchange in the Dialogue of the Savior[3] about the disciples choosing chastity and renouncing sexual relations. Judas asks, "When we pray, how should we pray?" The Lord answers, "Pray in the place where there is no woman." The disciple Matthew interprets this to mean "Destroy the works of womanhood," that is, cease giving birth. Mary Magdalene then says, "They will never be obliterated." Is she objecting? Is she standing up for "the works of womanhood?" It is possible, but she may also be going along with the discussion, voicing her pessimism that the physical and sexual are difficult to overcome. If this is correct, then Mary herself is shown giving "her approval to the use of gender imagery which emphasized women's inferiority and subordination typical of the dominant male construction of gender in Mediterranean society."[4]

In many of these texts, femaleness is something to be overcome or changed. In the First Apocalypse of James, femaleness is used to describe existence in this perishable material world. It is not to be obliterated or rejected, but transformed to the imperishable male element: "The perishable has [gone up] to the imperishable and the female element has attained to this male element."[5] In the Gospel of Thomas 114, Simon Peter says:

"Let Mary leave us, for women are not worthy of life." Jesus said, "I myself shall lead her in order to make her male, so that she too may become a living spirit [see Gen 2:7] resembling you males. For every woman who will make herself male will enter the kingdom of heaven."

What does it mean to say that Mary will be made male and that women should make themselves male? Does it mean dressing up like a man—cross-dressing and cutting one's hair short? There are examples of this kind of radical choice for women in the ancient world. In the Acts of Thecla, the heroine Thecla dresses up like a man. This keeps her safe as a traveler with Paul. In the Acts of Philip, Christ tells Mary, "[C]hange your dress and appearance: take off everything external to yourself that is reminiscent of a woman, the summer dress you are wearing."[6] This cross-dressing could be an act of self-defense, to minimize women's vulnerability in a hostile male world. But there is nothing in the Gospel of Thomas to indicate that "becoming male" means cross-dressing.

Perhaps "making oneself male" is a reference to the idea that the first human was originally androgynous (or a perfect combination of male and female). In Genesis 2, gender division only happens with the creation of Eve, *after* the creation of the first human. This could mean that to become "neither male nor female" (Thomas 22), like an androgyne, is what Jesus means by "becoming male." The problem with this view is that saying 114 uses the word for male (*hoout*) and not the word for human (*rōme*). Mary reaches her true spiritual self through maleness. The male disciples, apparently, have already become "living spirits," but they are still called "males" not humans or androgynes.

Perhaps the text of Thomas is rejecting gender difference altogether. In the thinking of the ancient world, "female" meant earthly, sensual, imperfect, and passive, while "male" meant transcendent, chaste, perfect, active, autonomous, rational, virtuous, and courageous. The movement of salvation for women and men, then, is from what is physical and earthly to that which is spiritual and heavenly. By making women male, gender difference is undone; if there is only one gender, there is no gender difference.

However it is interpreted, the goal of a woman "becoming male" reinforces traditional gender hierarchies of male over female, masculine over feminine. But the possibility that women can "become male" also disrupts these hierarchies, if only for a moment. Gender identity and gender difference are not fixed and thus can be manipulated. Some of the gnostic texts also disrupt gender expectations when they use female imagery for the divine powers. In the First Apocalypse of James, the Lord calls upon "the imperishable knowledge, which is Sophia who is in the Father [and] who is the mother of Achamoth." James is amazed that the seven women who are "[powerless] vessels have become strong by a perception which is in them."[7] Thus, the lines between male and female sometimes become quite blurry. In the Pistis Sophia, Mary says, "My man of light has guided [me], and has rejoiced and has welled up within me, wishing to come forth from me, and to go towards thee."[8] Has she become male? Is she a female giving birth to her male self? These questions are difficult to answer. In this text, the enlightened soul is identical to Jesus, but Jesus is a male christological figure who wears the "body" of the female divine.[9] Thus he is both male and female. There is a transgression here. Neither Mary nor Jesus is fully defined by their sexual identity.

The gnostic texts present a prominent Mary Magdalene who is named, speaks, and leads. She is also prominently opposed and rejected. As with many wo/men who have gained a reputation for insight and bold speech, Mary is contained, silenced, and limited by the kyriarchal texts in which she appears. Even the gnostic Mary requires feminist readers who will read against the grain of these texts and allow the disruptions and transgressions—not the andro-centrism—to have the last word.

Mary Speaks Boldly (#3), as a Visionary (#4), and with Superior Understanding (#5)

The gnostic Mary has a voice that is powerful, insistent, and coura-geous. In several texts, she enters into dialogue with Jesus, question-ing him and giving her own theological explanations. In the Pistis Sophia she asks to speak openly, and Jesus responds, "Mariam, thou blessed one, whom I will complete in all the mysteries of the height, speak openly." Her first question is theologically profound and con-cerns the Pistis Sophia, a divine power trapped in the physical world whose situation is like that of the disciples, male and female. Her interpretations are vigorous and technical; her questions direct, in-sistent, spunky. Usually she "springs up" to speak. Mary is called "spiritual one," and "beautiful in her speech." She seeks "every-thing with certainty and with accuracy." She is irrepressible, speaks for herself and the others. She speaks also about the mysteries of the Ineffable, and about community life—renouncing, preaching, and forgiving. When Jesus asks his disciples, "Do you understand in what manner I have spoken to you?" Mary answers, "Yes, O Lord, I have understood the discourse which thou hast spoken."[10]

Mary understands. She has direct contact with the Savior and this is the source of her knowledge (*gnosis*), her authority, and her teaching. In the Gospel of Philip, Mary is one of the three women who "always walked with the Lord."[11] In the Hebrew Bible, only Enoch and Noah are said to "walk with God" (Gen 5:24 and 6:9). In later Jewish tradition, Enoch and Noah are seen as visionaries. Thus, the use of this phrase "walked with God" implies that Mary is a visionary too. She is not one who receives private revelations and keeps them private, but one who experiences direct communication with the Savior and as a result has messages and insight for others.

In the Pistis Sophia, Mary both experiences and interprets visions. In one part, Mary and the other disciples see the risen Jesus engulfed in a great light reaching from earth to the heavens. Jesus rises to heaven in this light. In the ninth hour of the next day the heavens open and he descends in even more light, which he then turns off at the disciples' request. He begins to tell them what he has seen in his ascent to heaven. Mary is not said to have had a special, private vision, but later she stares into the air for one hour before she speaks.[12] She then uses Isaiah 19 to interpret the Savior's words about his defeat of the powers of the world.

In several instances, Mary's visionary experience is linked to mourning. Jesus' appearance to her in the Manichaean Psalm Book is a response to her tears and her grief. The risen Jesus says he did not appear to Mary "until I saw thy tears and thy grief."[13] In the Epistula Apostolorum 9–10, Mary and two other women carry ointment to pour on the dead body of Jesus, "weeping and mourning over what had happened." Not finding his body, "as they were mourning and weeping, the Lord appeared to them and said to them, do not weep; I am he whom you seek." The weeping and lamenting of Mary and her women friends in the Gospel of Peter 12–13 are also the occasion for an appearance, this time of a young man at the tomb.

Mary's understanding is recognized as superior insight and *gnosis*. In Dialogue of the Savior she is praised as "a woman who had understood completely." Mary says, "I want to understand all things, [just as] they are." In response to her request—"Tell me, Lord, why I have come to this place to profit or to forfeit"—she is praised by the

Lord: "You make clear the abundance of the revealer!"[14] In Pistis Sophia, Jesus says that "Mary Magdalene and John the virgin will surpass all my disciples and all men who shall receive mysteries in the Ineffable, they will be on my right hand and on my left, and I am they and they are I, and they will be equal with you in all things, save that your thrones will surpass theirs, and my own throne will surpass yours and those of all men who shall find the word of the Ineffable." Jesus gives a mark of "excellent" to almost every disciple who speaks, but Mary is praised enthusiastically and constantly by Jesus for her spiritual understanding. She is "blessed beyond all women on earth, because [she] shall be the pleroma of all pleromas and the completion of all completions," "blessed among all genera-tions." The Savior marvels at her answers—as he does at those of no others—"because she had completely become pure Spirit." Jesus says to her, "You are she whose heart is more directed to the Reign of Heaven than all your brothers."[15]

Mary's vision and insight is intellectual, spiritual, and emotional. Where all kinds of wo/men at that time were considered intellectu-ally inferior and morally deficient when compared to free men, Mary is the model gnostic who can see, hear, and understand the true nature of reality, salvation, and the divine world. Although it is too easy to say that the gnostic Mary was a role model for other women, she surely stands for us as an idealized example of wo/men's ability to break free of their social and religious roles and expectations.

Mary Is the Intimate Companion of Jesus (#6)

A lot of mileage has been made out of the implication in some gnostic texts that Mary and Jesus were intimate partners. The most famous example occurs in the Gospel of Philip. This passage is difficult to interpret and yet has caused much tantalizing debate:

> And the companion (*koinōnos*) of the [. . .] Mary Magdalene [. . .
> loved] her more than [all] the disciples [and used to] kiss her [often]
> on her [. . .]. The rest of [the disciples . . .]. They said to him,
> "Why do you love her more than all of us?" The Savior answered
> and said to them, "Why do I not love you like her?"[16]

Earlier in the text, Mary is called Jesus' companion. She is one of the "three who always walked with the Lord: Mary his mother, her sister and the Magdalene, the one who was called his companion (*tef-koinōnos*)."[17] She is not called the "companion" of the Lord anywhere else in the gnostic literature, and no one else is called his "companion."

What does it mean to say Mary is Jesus' companion? The Greek term *koinōnos* has a wide range of meanings in the Bible and elsewhere: marriage partner, participant, co-worker in evangelization, companion in faith, business partner, comrade, friend. The notion of sharing interests, enterprises, material possessions, education, and meals is central to it. It is possible that the text presents Mary Magdalene as Jesus' earthly partner. As Elisabeth Schüssler Fiorenza points out, Valentinian gnostics "knew three Christs and perceived the divine and the world in syzygies (couples)." Thus it may be that Mary Magdalene was paired with the earthly Jesus, and the Holy Spirit was the partner of the divine Christ, and Sophia was the consort of the Savior.[18]

Jesus and Mary's union—perhaps physical, surely spiritual—could function as an example of the ideal couple that the gnostic Christians should try to imitate. It is debated whether or not this sort of partnership—between Jesus and Mary Magdalene and thus between the male and female gnostics—involves actual marriage and/or sexual intercourse. Some scholars say that this text promotes celibacy even in marriage. Others argue that sexual intercourse is required for the spiritual union sought by the true gnostic. Elaine Pagels thinks that the Gospel of Philip is intentionally ambiguous and mysterious on this point. The author, she says, refuses to join the conversation among second-century Christians about sexual practice. This ambiguity in the text calls its readers to a maturity that gets beyond the false dichotomy of marriage versus celibacy. The text is more interested, says Pagels, in how to reconcile the freedom gnosis brings with relational love.[19]

This interpretation of Mary Magdalene's companionship with Jesus as ambiguous and enigmatic strikes me as extremely important and profound. Such ambiguity avoids two alternatives that both accept and perpetuate typical notions of the female body: (1) that any male-female relationship must involve sexual relations; or (2) that "sacred" or "spiritual" male-female relations must not be sexual.[20] This ambiguity is not easy to hold on to because the whorish legend of the Magdalene is hard to shake. It is difficult to imagine Jesus and Mary together without thinking about sex or to see their spiritual intimacy as deeply erotic. I am using erotic here in the way that Audre Lorde does—as a deep source of power, knowledge, joy, bravery, and the energy to change the world.[21]

Clearly, the gnostic texts portray an intimacy between Jesus and Mary. In the Gospel of Philip, Jesus is said to love Mary Magdalene more than all the disciples and to "kiss her [often] on her [. . . .]" That last gap teases us; how is it to be filled? With mouth? lips? head? hand? feet? The passage exists at present in only this one flawed manuscript (Codex II from Nag Hammadi). Evidence in the Gospel of Philip itself suggests that mouth is the best choice. In 59,

1–6, talk of nourishment from the mouth is linked to the kiss by which "the perfect conceive and give birth . . . from the grace which is in one another." The kiss could be a metaphor of spiritual inter-course, or a sign for sexual intercourse. The Gospel of Philip never denies that kissing may have a literal sense; but another section shows that it clearly has a metaphorical meaning:

> And the word had gone out from that heavenly place, it would be nourished from the mouth and it would become perfect. For it is by a kiss that the perfect conceive and give birth. For this reason we also kiss one another. We receive conception from the grace, which is in one another.[22]

Karen King gives three possible understandings of this metaphorical kissing. Either it is "(1) a reference to teaching through the word; (2) a metaphor for an intimate and personal reception of the word of teaching; or (3) the Christian practice of the kiss of fellowship."[23] One or all of these may be intended when Jesus "kisses" Mary in the Gospel of Philip. This means that Mary is seen as one who accepted and understood his teaching and was therefore loved by him.

So the kiss too is ambiguous, enigmatic. Asking whether this is either a spiritual love between a master and disciple, or an erotic love creates a false dichotomy that is rooted in the Christian tradi-tion's separation of bodily things (like sexuality) from spiritual things (like religion itself). The gnostic Mary's spiritual/erotic inti-macy with Jesus is the opposite of the western Magdalene legend in which Jesus chastely rescues Mary from a demonic life of sex and sexuality.

Mary Leads the Male Disciples (#7) Who Both Oppose (#8) and Defend Her (#9)

The gnostic Mary is someone who shows others the way. Her leadership does not always mean that Mary has followers, that she is successful, or that she has power to go with her authority. Rather she is shown comforting and encouraging the others to move on, correcting them, urging them to believe and act. In the Pistis Sophia, Mary functions as a team-teacher with Jesus. In the Manichean Psalm Book she is a fisher of men: "A net-caster is Mary (Marihama), hunting for the eleven others that were wandering."[24] She is commissioned to go to the "wandering orphans," using "all [her] skill and advice" to bring "the sheep to the shepherd," the Risen Jesus. She is not only to deliver a message, but to make sure it is understood. She accepts the commission with dedication and enthusiasm, becoming the model gnostic. In the Acts of Philip, Mary stands beside Christ when he commissions his apostles, and encourages her brother Philip who is moaning and weeping about the city to which he is sent. She holds the register of the regions to be evangelized, and prepares the bread and salt and the breaking of the bread. She is told to accompany Philip. Dressed as a man, she does so and stands by him when he is martyred.

But Mary's intellectual and spiritual leadership is regularly opposed by various male disciples. In the Gospel of Philip they ask, "Why do you love her more than all of us?" Jesus' response turns the question around to focus on them: "Why do I not love you like her?" The little parable that follows indirectly answers the question: "When a blind man and one who sees are both together in darkness, they are no different from one another. When the light comes, then he who sees will see the light, and he who is blind will remain in darkness."[25] The parable depicts Mary as able to see the light and the disciples as blind. He loves her because she is different, she has spiritual insight and ability they do not have.

Peter opposes Mary in the Pistis Sophia. When asked if the disciples understand Jesus' teachings, Peter leaps forward and says: "My Lord, we are not able to suffer this woman who takes the opportunity from us, and does not allow anyone of us to speak, but she speaks many times." Peter here protests for all the males, accusing Mary of denying them opportunity, and attributing to her the power to silence them. Jesus comforts Peter, invites him to speak, and praises him when he does: "Well done, Peter. . . . You are blessed beyond all men upon earth, for I have revealed to you these mysteries."[26]

Peter's opposition affects Mary. She later says: "My Lord, my mind is understanding at all times that I should come forward and give the interpretation of the words which [Pistis Sophia] spoke, but I am afraid of Peter, for he threatens me and hates our race."[27] She is afraid not only for herself, but for the "race" (*genos*) of women. The First Mystery (Jesus) replies, "Everyone who will be filled with the Spirit of light to come forward and give the interpretation of those things which I say, him will no one be able to prevent." Mary is told to give her interpretation, and she so does several more times in the text.

But Peter's anger also seems to have made Mary more guarded with Jesus. In one section she gives a rather neurotic-sounding rationalization for herself: you told us to ask, there is no one else to ask but you, we ask out of spiritual knowledge! Jesus answers her, "Question that which thou dost wish to question, and I will reveal it with assurance and certainty." But in the very next chapter, she is springing up to say again, "My Lord, be not angry with me for questioning thee, for we question all things with assurance." Several times she tries to ward off of Jesus' anger. He repeatedly responds that she should ask what she wants, and he will reveal it openly.[28]

But Peter still thinks she talks too much. In Pistis Sophia IV, he says: "My Lord, let the women cease to question, that we also may question." Unlike the beginning of this text, Jesus now says to Mary and the women, "Give way to the men, your brothers, that they may question also." Mary does not stop questioning as Peter wanted, but as the advanced star pupil she is slowed down and restrained so that the other students can catch up. She does not speak again until after Peter, Andrew, Thomas, Bartholomew, and John have asked their questions. All Mary's questions, all her springing up to speak, all that vitality is over.

In the gnostic texts Peter appears envious, contentious, and misogynistic. The tension between Peter and Mary does not usually involve doctrinal issues. It is about the position of Mary within the group of disciples, her right to act as a spiritual and intellectual authority, her right to take the lead, to represent. In the Gospel of Thomas, Peter's concerns about Mary apply to all women. He says, "Women are not worthy of life" (114). In fact, in many texts outside the Christian Testament, the figure of Peter is associated with hostility toward women. He is portrayed in one version of the Acts of Philip as a man who "fled from all places where there was a woman."[29] In the fifth-century ascetic work, the Pseudo-Titus Epistle, Peter is shown eliminating the sexual threat of a young girl by his prayer "that the Lord bestow on her what is expedient for her soul." She drops dead. In the Acts of Peter, he also causes his own daughter to become paralyzed in order to preserve her virginity: "For this [daughter] will wound many souls if her body remains healthy."[30]

Who defends Mary? In the Manichaean Psalm Book, it is Jesus who coaches Mary on how to change her message when it is scorned. In the Epistula Apostolorum 11, Jesus himself goes with the women in the third attempt to tell of the resurrection; he rebukes Peter for denying him again (presumably by not believing the women, who, however, disappear from the story before the male disciples believe). Jesus overtly comes to Mary's defense in the Gospel of Thomas 114: "Look, I will lead her that I may make her male, in order that she too may become a living spirit resembling you males." Is this a full-fledged defense with its talk of making Mary male? Is Jesus accepting Peter's terms like he does in Pistis Sophia when he tells the women to give way to the men?

These ambiguous defenses stand in contrast to Levi's defense of Mary in the Gospel of Mary (discussed in the next section) and Jesus's instructive little parable in the Gospel of Philip 55. The parable speaks of all, the blind and the sighted, being no different from one another in the darkness. But in the light, the blind remain blind, and the sighted see. If the disciples' question concerns gender issues, by implying perhaps that as a woman she should be loved less, the defense levels the field. "Why do I not love you like her?" is an invitation to self-reflection. The parable suggests that as the sighted see in the light, the loveable (spiritually talented?) are loved—regardless of their gender.

Does Mary ever defend herself? Not directly, except perhaps in one text. In the Apostolic Church Order, the topic under discussion—raised by Peter—is whether the Eucharistic ministry should be open to women. John answers that it should not because women were not permitted to stand at the last supper. Then Martha explains that, "It was because of Mary, because he saw her smiling." This is the only instance in gnostic literature in which a woman appears hostile to Mary. The Magdalene seems to defend herself against the charge, responding that she did not laugh (or no longer laughed). Mary explains that Jesus taught that "the weak [women] will be saved through the strong [men]." Here there is no boldness, as she takes back her laughter and speaks for the secondary status of women.

In each example where women and men assert gendered hierarchies or use androcentric language for salvation and knowledge, one can see that becoming an insider, with access to social identity, order, power, salvation, has a high price for women. The profile of a gnostic Mary Magdalene does not settle contemporary debates about women in early and contemporary Christianity, but she does give us a glimpse of the ongoing struggle for alternatives to the dichotomous choice between a woman as a Virgin or a Whore.

The Gospel of Mary

Originally written in Greek in the late first or early second century CE, the Gospel of Mary was not found at Nag Hammadi. It is preserved only in three fragmentary copies: a Coptic translation, and two Greek papyri from Oxyrhynchus in Egypt. It has ten or more missing pages (over half the work) and many gaps. Comparison of the Coptic and the Greek indicates that objections raised about Mary originally focused on the content of her teaching, and later on her being a woman. The depiction of Mary Magdalene in the Gospel of Mary provides a full-bodied version of the gnostic profile presented in bits and pieces above.

The first six pages of this work are missing and the text begins in the middle of a post-resurrection dialogue between the Savior and the disciples concerning matter ("Will matter then be utterly destroyed or not?") and sin ("What is the sin of the world?"). After commissioning them to "Go then, preach the good news of the Realm," the risen Savior "departs."

> The disciples were distressed and wept greatly. "How are we going to go out to the rest of the world to preach the good news about the Realm of the child of true Humanity?" they said. "If they did not spare him, how will they spare us?" Then Mary stood up. She greeted them all, addressing her brothers and sisters, "Do not weep and be distressed nor let your hearts be irresolute. For his grace will be with you all and will shelter you. Rather we should praise his greatness, for he has united us [or prepared us] and made us true Human beings." When Mary said these things, she turned their mind [or heart] toward the Good, and they began to debate about the words of the Savior. Peter said to Mary, "Sister, we know that the Savior loved you more than any other woman. Tell us the words of the Savior that you know but which we haven't heard." Mary responded, "I will report to you as much as I remember that is unknown to you." And she began to speak these words to them. She said, "I saw the Lord in a vision and I said to him, 'Lord, I saw you today in a vision.' He answered me 'How wonderful you are for not wavering at seeing me! For where the mind is, there is the treasure.' I said to him, 'So now, Lord, does a person who sees a vision see it—with the soul or with the spirit?' The Savior answered, 'A <person or visionary> does not see with the soul or with the spirit. Rather the mind, which exists between these two—sees the vision and that is what. . . .'"[31]

Four pages are missing at this point. The text resumes in the midst of a description by Mary of the ascent of the soul past the four powers (the four elements of matter), the last of which takes seven forms (representing the seven astrological spheres), "the seven Powers of Wrath." When this goal is achieved, the soul says, "From now on, for the rest of the course of the [due] measure of the time of the age, I will rest in silence."

After Mary's speech about the soul's ascent, her words are challenged by the disciples:

> After Mary had said these things, she was silent, since it was up to this point that the Savior had spoken to her. Andrew said, "Brothers, what is your opinion of what was just said? Indeed I do not believe that the Savior said these things, for what she said appears to give views that are different from his thought." After examining these matters, <Peter said,> "Has the Savior spoken secretly to a woman and <not> openly so that we would all hear? Surely he did not want to show that she is more worthy than we are?" Then Mary wept and said to Peter, "My brother Peter, what are you imagining? Do you think that I have thought up these things by myself in my heart or that I am telling lies about the Savior?" Levi said to Peter, "Peter, you are always ready to give way to your perpetual inclination to anger. And even now you are doing exactly that by questioning the woman as though you are her adversary. If the Savior considered her to be worthy, who are you to disregard her? For he knew her completely <and> loved her steadfastly. Rather we should be ashamed and, once we clothe ourselves with the perfect Human, we should do what we were commanded. We should announce the good news as the Savior said, and not be laying down any rules or making laws." After he said these things, Levi left <and> began to announce the good news.[32]

Mary's prominence is indicated by her standing in the assembly to address the quaking, grieving disciples. Although the language is male-centered (literally: "son of man" in 4:5; "he has . . . made us into men" in 5:8; "put on the perfect man" in 10:11), Karen King translates inclusively ("child of true humanity" in 4:5; "true Human beings" in 5:8; and "perfect Human" in 10:11). I agree with this translation because in this text the meaning is clearly inclusive. I see no indication that the viewpoint of the author is sexist, that men are valued more than women, or that in order to become true human beings women must overcome their femaleness more than men must overcome their maleness. In fact, different from the Gospel of Thomas, that viewpoint is explicitly rejected.

Mary's initial speech in the Gospel of Mary boldly names the disciples' emotional states: they grieve, they weep, they are irresolute or doubtful. She promises the Savior's grace will shelter them, and calls them to know themselves as joined together, made true human beings. She calls them, that is, to a sense of their present unity and power, rather than to a hope of perfection and strength in some future time. Later, Peter asks Mary to teach what she knows but what the others have not heard. She does so willingly, describing a conversation with the Lord about her vision of him; she asks him about visions, how they work.

Mary's leadership is clear at the beginning of the Gospel, as she takes over the Savior's role when he departs. Comforting and encouraging them (and in the Greek, tenderly kissing each of them), she turns their mind toward the Good. Her leadership at first seems to be accepted by the males who begin to ask her about the words of the Savior. Peter acknowledges that the Savior loved her, and that she knows words of the Savior that they do not know, and he asks her to tell them. When her teaching is challenged, Levi's intervention on her behalf validates her leadership—for himself at least, in the Greek text, as he leaves alone on the mission; for all, in the Coptic text, as they leave together to teach and to preach.

Mary is represented as not knowing how one experiences visions, as she asks the Savior if it is with the soul or with the spirit. The Savior tells her the vision is seen with the mind (*nous*), which is between the soul and spirit, and acts as a mediator between the senses and the divine spirit. The visionary experience is not understood as penetration by a spirit or loss of control. The information about the ascent of the soul is information she is relaying from the Savior; it may be information from her own mind's experience, of following the child of true humanity within her. The missing pages prevent us from knowing exactly whose ascent is being described. Surely the point of Mary telling the disciples about her vision of the Lord, and about the teaching on ascent, is to move them to vision and *gnosis*, to set them on that ascent. As a seer, she presents a vision of unity, for which she is opposed.

The Savior praises Mary for "not wavering at seeing me" in her vision. Her mind is stable, fixed on the eternal and spiritual. Peter's request acknowledges her as a teacher, the favorite woman. Mary responds that she will report what she remembers (the Coptic of 6:3 makes it clearer that Mary has secret knowledge: "I will teach you about what is hidden from you"). In the existing text, the teaching that Mary gives is not in conflict with the teaching of the Savior about matter and sin in chapters 2–4, but Andrew accuses her of having opinions different from the Savior's. In Levi's defense of her, he says, "If the Savior considered her to be worthy, who are you to disregard her? For he knew her completely <and> loved her steadfastly." The Coptic of 10:10 reads, "Assuredly the Savior's knowledge of her is completely reliable. That is why he loved her more than us." She is not praised by the men for her understanding, but the Savior's knowledge of her is thought by Levi—and perhaps by the author—to validate it.

Peter acknowledges that the Savior loved Mary "more than all other women." Love in this work is based on intimate knowledge, mind to mind. The love has no overtly sexual overtones: it is basically a recognition of spiritual maturity. But after hearing Mary teach, Peter is incensed at the thought that the Savior might have spoken secretly to her, and that this might be an indication that she "is more worthy than we are." She knows too much. The Coptic heightens what he sees as an absurdity: "Did he, then, speak with a woman in private without our knowing about it? Are we to turn around and listen to her? Did he choose her over us?" Peter is able to accept Mary as the most loved woman, but not as the chosen or most loved person/disciple.[33] This is a power struggle.

The logic of the hostility Mary faces is hard to follow. It is clear that Andrew is unconvinced by her teaching. In the Coptic he declares: "Say what you will about the things she has said, but I do not believe that the Savior said these things, for indeed these teachings are strange ideas!" Her words are unacceptable to him not only because they are different from the Savior's, but also because they are strange in themselves. They come from somewhere else. But there is no discussion of their origin or their substance.

From what we have of the document, the words of Mary are not strange, nor are they different from the Savior's. The teachings of the Savior at the beginning of this work have to do with the dissolving, interconnected nature of matter, and with freeing oneself from the body and following after "the child of true humanity" that exists within each person. Mary's teachings are an application or example of this: the soul follows, searching within and traveling through the realms of the Powers (Darkness, Desire, Ignorance, Wrath), conquering attachment to the world and therefore the fear of death, and ultimately reaching rest. Andrew's objections seem like an early charge of false prophecy and "heresy." Perhaps he is hostile to her teachings because they are hers.

Peter's objection makes the hostility to Mary explicit. He questions the idea that the Savior would have spoken secretly to a woman, rather than openly to all. The contrast here is not only between secret speech and open speech, but also between secret speech to a woman and speech of any kind to the males. Secret teaching to a woman is unthinkable because it might indicate that she is more worthy than them or that he chose her over them. Peter's questions are rhetorical. The attack is not personal; Mary is not attacked as unworthy, unmarried, unveiled, demon-possessed, impure, or whatever—but as a woman.

Mary does not respond to Andrew, but she is hurt by Peter's attack and weeps. She defends herself in a conciliatory manner, without anger, calling Peter "brother" as he had earlier called her "sister." She asks if he thinks she made it all up or that she is telling lies about the Savior. Her defense relies on Peter's good assessment of her character and Peter's good will toward her. But he does not know her, and his good will does not exist.

Levi's defense of Mary is a counterattack on Peter's character: "You are always ready to give way to your perpetual inclination to anger" (Coptic: "You have always been a wrathful person"). Levi sees Peter's objection as an expression of his anger, "questioning the woman as if you are her adversary." Levi's defense rests on the Savior's evaluation of Mary. This is the only time in all surviving ancient literature that Peter is criticized when Mary is defended. Levi does not address the issue of Mary as a woman, but he does call for the disciples to be ashamed. He brings them back to the Savior's last words, telling them to clothe themselves with that perfect Human that the Savior had said exists within them. They were to follow it, search for it, and find it. Levi reminds them they were to go and preach the good news "and not be laying down any rules or making laws." I can imagine the rules or laws just under the surface of what Peter had said: women's spiritual experience is to be subject to male approval and control. Women will not teach men. Women will not lead men. Women will not claim roles the Savior did not give them. Men will be in charge of determining the authenticity of all teaching about the Savior, whether based on memory and interpretation of his career and person, or on subsequent experience.

Andrew, Peter, and the other males do not reply to Levi, who departs alone (contrast the Coptic where "they began to go forth" but without assenting to Mary's teaching or Levi's defense of it). Levi is a "true human" who recognizes Mary as one too. Levi is a better "man" than analytical, narrow Andrew and bullying, aggressive Peter. Levi uses his privileged position to stand up against Peter. Masculinities and femininities are in the process of being deconstructed here.

The ending of this Gospel is ambiguous, and the controversy is far from resolved, but it has let us hear some of the voices of those who spoke for women's leadership in ancient Christianity. Lost for centuries, the Gospel of Mary is one of those rediscovered texts that seriously challenges the canon. Unencumbered by complex gnostic systems and terminology, it is accessible to all contemporary readers. The gaps are opportunities for creativity whether or not the missing pages are ever found.

The codex was found in a burial place near Akhmim in Egypt. Who placed it there, and with whose body? I wouldn't mind having it buried with me too, with my ashes. On a disc or whatever is technologically available. I'd like to hear its words ring out in Christian—especially Catholic—assemblies: "If the Savior considered her to be worthy, who are you to disregard her?" The question "Who are you?" is a call for *gnosis*.

From Gnostic Mary to Early Christians

What can be said about early Christian women's lives based on these texts? On the one hand, the elevated role given to Mary Magdalene in the Gospel of Mary and elsewhere in gnostic or near-gnostic literature might represent the authoritative roles of women (such as prophet, teacher, healer, priest, bishop) in some—not all—actual gnostic communities, in which women and men might have been considered equal. That would mean that Mary Magdalene was chosen as a major character and speaker in part because she was a woman. She was presented as one on whose memory later women based their successful claims to power in some communities. Or, on the other hand, one could say that the negative references to femaleness in the gnostic sources indicate that women were devalued and subordinated in gnostic communities. Femaleness was reduced to a focus on sexuality and procreation, and warnings were issued against both. It would be unlikely, then, with this emphasis that women functioned as bishops or priests or enjoyed high status in real gnostic groups. As with life itself, the whole situation is very complex.

Mary, whether representing "woman" as a stage to be left behind as in the Gospel of Thomas 114, or identified with earthly/otherworldly creative entities as in the Gospel of Philip, or speaking sanely, charismatically, and compassionately as in the Gospel of Mary, is a paradigm of the saved. She must have been interpreted in a wide variety of ways by the saved. In some texts, her appearance leads to reflection about the position of women in general (Peter "hates our race"); in other texts there is no such reflection. Sometimes the depiction of her energy and intelligence contrasts strongly with ancient notions about the weakness of the female. The rivalry between Mary and Peter may reflect the debate between different groups of Christians, or a debate internal to one group. Some gnostic Christians may have spoken out, in the name of Mary, about visionary traditions, their own experience, their own reasoning, their own reading of the past.

There is a clear recognition in these texts of injustice, of hostility faced by women, of the dismissive scorn with which some men treated them. Some men, weakly or strongly, might have defended women thinking and speaking, and defended women's presence and leadership. There seems to have been some perception of what we would call the social construction of gender and its fluidity. Women are spoken of as being made male, becoming male, becoming human. This perception is one-sided, since there is no clear corresponding change imagined for males. The presence in the same texts of a Mary who is enlightened and strong, and of language that absorbs or assimilates the female into the male, shows that we are not dealing in any of the texts with egalitarianism* in any full sense. But some of the evidence provides glimpses of egalitarianism struggling within a system or systems that cannot accommodate it: glimpses of women in positions of authority within dualistic, kyriarchal systems. Even when gnostic antifeminism, sexism, misogyny, and androcentrism are recognized, there are still indications in the texts of more powerful roles for women in some gnostic circles. Mary, like other female figures in gnostic texts, is often charged with sexual power, and with female power to act and create.

In sum, the hypothesis that Mary reflects the more extensive roles women played in gnostic communities, as leaders and as sources of revelation and authority, is a hypothesis increasingly seen as difficult to test, yet worthy of exploration. Also difficult to test, yet demanding exploration, is the hypothesis that these gnostic women's roles are related in some way to roles for women in the *basileia* movement, themselves rooted in egalitarian forms of Judaism. As discussed in the next chapter, the struggle for egalitarianism requires some sort of vision, some ideal, however vaguely or inadequately articulated. I find that vision and ideal expressed in language about the child of true Humanity or the Human One, which threads through the book of Daniel, the Christian Testament, and apocryphal works like the Gospel of Mary.

From Gnostic Mary to Canonical Mary

The Mary Magdalene of the Christian Testament is quite unlike the gnostic and apocryphal Mary. In the Christian Gospels, she is important, but not prominent. Like all the characters other than Jesus, she speaks very little; in her case, only to the figures at the empty tomb, to the risen Jesus, and then to the disciples about the resurrection, except in Mark where she is said to remain silent out of fear. She has no role encouraging the disciples, is not said to be a visionary, is never praised, is not said to be a leader. She is not called the companion of Jesus, and in the Gospel of John the "beloved disciple" is a male. Though disbelieved by all the disciples as a whole in Luke, she is never challenged by Peter or any other individual male. She is never defended, nor does she defend herself.

Entering the world of the Christian Testament is entering a world that is both strange and too familiar, a world loud with women's silence. Of course, it cannot be a completely different world. In the next chapter, I try to drive from here to that other world, to which at this time there are no well-traveled roads. The Mary(s) of the "heretics" are related in ways that are not yet clear to both the repentant whore of legend and to the demon-possessed, exorcised woman of the Christian Testament. The historian must not be limited by the borders of canon, and must not see the canon as always and everywhere preserving earlier or better tradition. The Gospel of Mary and other works may preserve very early tradition that has been filtered out of the canonical materials.

This presentation of gnostic and apocryphal Mary traditions has been extensive. I have tried to make chunks of the actual texts available to readers, to show by contrast the narrowness of and puzzling gaps in the canonical depiction of Mary Magdalene, and to give a sense of the struggles that resulted in the distortion, destruction, and erasure of women's traditions and the eventual exclusions of women from positions of authority. Flawed as she is as a proponent and symbol of egalitarianism, the gnostic Mary interrupts the voices of the Christian Testament and the Church Fathers. As she speaks boldly from the outside, she can teach us to read the canonical texts in new ways.

CHAPTER 4

The Women Did Not Flee

> I am not concerned with the single life, but with lives together. I have—am trying to find, in the folds of the past, such fragments as time having broken the perfect vessel, still keeps safe. The perfect vessel? But it was not by any means made of durable stuff. For it was only when the thing had happened and the violence of the shock was over that one could understand, or really live.
>
> VIRGINIA WOOLF
> Draft of *The Waves*

FINALLY ARRIVING at the Christian Testament, dazzled, annoyed, and bemused by the rich array of Mary's legendary and non-canonical afterlife, it is hard not to be disappointed by the sketchy portrait of her in the Bible. If she is not the woman who anoints Jesus, the woman caught in adultery, or Martha's sister sitting at Jesus' feet, what is left of her? Only a few things: a couple of brief reports tell that she was part of the group around Jesus in Galilee and followed him from there to Jerusalem. In all four Gospels a group of women witness the crucifixion and visit Jesus' tomb after his death. Three of the Gospels tell how Mary is sent to explain the empty tomb to the disciples. In Matthew, John, and a later version of Mark, Mary

Magdalene is the first to experience a vision of the resurrected Jesus. Mary speaks only in the Gospel of John. Historians face this hard fact: the Christian Testament texts tell us almost nothing about Mary Magdalene beyond her steadfast presence at the crucial points in the story of the career, death, and resurrection of Jesus.

We could stop here. We could say that the historical Mary Magdalene is, like the site at Migdal, lost irretrievably. Let her memory serve as a warning: wo/men were made outsiders to Christianity from the very beginning. We do not know them unless they were somehow related to an important man. Alternatively, we could turn instead to the legends, embrace their fictions and release their energies through re-telling and re-creation. Listen to prostitutes organizing and reclaiming Mary's story. Study her powerfully erotic image in art and literature and music. Give her full voice in drama and film. Or, we could retrieve the gnostic Mary. Make an alliance between her and the Christian Testament Mary, who at least some texts say was the first to witness the resurrection. Put these Marys to work supporting contemporary efforts to reform Christianity.

There are scholars of the Christian Testament who say that its fragmentary and diminished depiction of Mary is all there is, that anything else is wishful thinking. But feminist readers of the Christian Testament assume there was more going on than the texts show—that women were there. When the male disciples flee for fear in the face of Jesus' crucifixion, the women do not flee. We owe them the same steadfastness: to search for them, to say what can be said, and to stand by as witnesses when their memories are truly lost.

What *can* be said about the Christian Testament texts that mention Mary Magdalene? Here is the whole list: Mark 15:40–41 and 47, 16:1–8, and 16:9–11 (from the longer ending of Mark, see below); Matthew 27:55–56 and 61, and 28:1–10; Luke 8:1–3, 23:49,

55–56, and 24:1–11; and finally, John 19:25, and 20:1–18. All the Gospels agree on four things about Mary: (1) that she was part of the group around Jesus; (2) that she was present at his crucifixion; (3) that she visited Jesus' tomb and found it empty; and (4) that she received a vision, either of an angel or of Jesus himself. If we look closely, can we catch a glimpse of the historical Mary?

Confident historical facts about the Magdalene are surely lost to us. Writing history, however, is not finding facts but rather making informed and carefully defended proposals and hypotheses. I cannot shut the door or close the case on speculation about the historical Magdalene. I would not want to do that. Rather, I will try to open doors, imagine historical possibilities, describe what is plausible in order to shape what is thinkable. That is all history ever really is, but historians do not like to admit it. They work with certain assumptions, but do not acknowledge that either. As a feminist historian, I approach the search for Mary and for early Christian wo/men from a particular point of view. I place wo/men's lives at the center of my investigations. I assume they were active people, busy shaping and interpreting their world. Because wo/men have always struggled against their own oppression and silencing, I look for signs of their resistance, creativity, and contribution to a vision for change. I have questioned and rejected reconstructions that deny the possibility of wo/men's presence and agency in the early Christian movement. I have accepted probabilities and reconstructions that allow for it. Because the text and its interpreters often hide the wo/men, I read between the lines or against the grain of the text to make them visible.

If you think about the simple and enduring fact that wo/men have always been active in the human community, then the burden of proof is really on those who want to say that women were *not* shapers of early Christianity. I think that they were and that we can use historical imagination to put them back into the story. This chapter looks carefully at the four areas related to all of the Magdalene texts: the "reign of God" or *basileia* movement, the cross, the empty tomb, and the appearances. The next chapter proposes some new ways to read the distinctive story of Mary's vision of the resurrected Jesus in the Gospel of John.

The Basileia *Movement of Jesus and His Companions*

Mary Magdalene and other women are said to have associated with Jesus in Galilee (Luke 8:1–3) and traveled from there to Jerusalem (Mark 14:41; Matthew 27:55; Luke 23:49, 55). How did they participate in the group? Did they travel about like Jesus and the male disciples or did they offer support when Jesus visited settled towns? Did they contribute to the healing ministry and table fellowship like some men or did they provide domestic services or even financial support as wealthy patrons? Were they motivated by gratitude for personal healing as implied in Luke or did they understand themselves as receiving a call? To what extent did their needs, insights, and questions shape the movement? How one answers these questions influences how we understand the nature of the movement that coalesced around Jesus and his co-workers and companions.

Following Elisabeth Schüssler Fiorenza, I call this the *basileia* movement. In the Gospels, Jesus often speaks of the "kingdom" or "reign" of God. I understand this idea as invoking a sacred vision of a radical alternative to human systems of domination, a religiously inspired dream of the way the world would be, might be, and could be. It resists, disrupts, and envisions alternatives to the way the world too often was and is: unjust, hierarchical, and violent. Like Schüssler Fiorenza, I prefer to leave the Greek word *basileia* (pro-

nounced ba-si-lay-uh) untranslated when referring to this movement. By speaking of the *basileia* of God, instead of "kingdom," I
keep the idea that this is a political vision (*basileia* is a word for
domain, or imperial rule, or realm), but I also try to disrupt imagining God in the male-centered and politically hierarchical language
of human kingship.

In my view, the *basileia* movement was egalitarian, in the sense
that women as well as men were full members and active partici-
pants (though they are not clearly depicted as such in the Gospels).
There was an implied, but not fully expressed ideal of equality moti-
vating the movement, which can be detected in the texts. A close
reading of the Gospels suggests that the movement around Jesus did
not explicitly attack the power structures that create injustice and
oppression, but implicitly subverted them "by envisioning a different future and different human relationships on the grounds that all
persons in Israel are created and elected by the gracious goodness of
Jesus' Sophia-God."[1] Historically this was not a unique or perfect
egalitarian community. Rather, it was like any movement for
change: men and women in community, struggling toward a vision.
Precisely because it was imperfect, incomplete, unfinished, indeter-
minate, it is a resource for the future. As Gloria Steinem once said,
"We are all in transition to an equality no one has ever known."[2]

Of course, there is evidence to support this view that the movement of Jesus and his companions was egalitarian. It is sometimes
difficult to find more than hints of egalitarianism in the Bible, but
those hints are present. Women were clearly members of the movement. Table fellowship was inclusive. Some women were with Jesus
in Galilee and followed him up to Jerusalem; others, like Mary and
Martha of Bethany, seem to have been members who did not travel
with him. Some may have traveled with him at times, stayed home
at other times. Those who stayed at home—both men and

women—probably provided crucial roles as local leaders of the movement in villages.

This was a kind of ancient liberation movement, resisting the domination of Roman and probably Temple establishments, focused on intertwined political, economic, social, and theological issues. There were several such movements in this period of Judaism: John the Baptist's movement, the Therapeutae in Egypt, revolutionary and apocalyptic groups, Pharisaic table-fellowships, and perhaps the Qumran community at the edge of the Dead Sea. It is important to remember these Jewish groups because today's Christians too often imagine that Jesus and Christianity uniquely rescued Jewish women from the oppression of Judaism. But as the Jewish feminist Judith Plaskow puts it, Jesus "is never portrayed as arguing for women's prerogatives, demanding changes in particular restrictive laws that affect women, or debating the Pharisees on the subject of gender." Jesus should be seen as "simply a Jewish man who treated women like people . . . [who] acted respectfully toward women without ever explicitly defending their cause. . . . [H]is attitudes toward women would represent not a victory over early Judaism but a possibility within it."[3] Jewish women probably joined the movement of Jesus and his companions, or any of these movements, because of the situations that Jews of both genders and all social circumstances faced in the first century. Roman domination, Herodian corruption, and the Temple system all put various pressures on people. All kinds of women—not only Jewish women—struggled under societal norms of gender inequality and roles.

Although the Christian Testament provides no evidence that Jesus was an outspoken feminist in the contemporary sense, or that he was unique for his time and place in his treatment of women, there is ample evidence that the participation of women in the movement drew criticism and control, women were pushed aside and their traditions were sometimes eliminated or distorted in the earliest communities; there is evidence, in other words, of struggle. The Gospels' lack of treatment of gender issues and their meager and sometimes negative depictions of women give evidence of that struggle.

The possibility of egalitarianism within Judaism is rooted in the belief, always struggling to be realized, that the entire people of Israel are God's children. Everyone is to be trained in the nature of justice, and must know its history of freedom from enslavement, and its own rights and duties (Deut 31:9–13). Nehemiah 8 commands the public reading of the teaching of Moses every seven years before all the people, "all Israel"—men, women, children, and resident aliens. In later rabbinic times, this was expanded into a year-round system of reading the Torah aloud in the synagogue. Private teaching in the family is urged (see Deut 4:9–10; 5:1; 6:6–9, 20–25; 11:18–20). Because of the elite male control of the teachings and their interpretation, it might be argued that such education functioned to keep women subordinate; but it must have had leveling power as well. Whether or not women served as leaders in Galilean villages and synagogues in the time of Jesus, they probably participated actively in them and made their own contributions.

The idea of a community that included both men and women was also present in other Jewish groups of the period. The Therapeutae in Egypt seem to have included women and men on an equal or near equal basis, and both shared fully in the community celebrations. Unlike the *basileia* movement around Jesus, however, their scripture study did not, as far as we know, lead them to lives of social involvement. As for the communities connected with Qumran, Eileen Schuller holds that women's full membership may be presumed, in the absence of evidence to the contrary, and in the presence of evidence that may support this.[4] The ancient Jewish historian Josephus says Simon ben Giora had "a following of women" that included Simon's wife and her female servants.[5] No Jewish sources portray women as disciples in early rabbinic circles, but the fact that there is debate in those sources over whether and under what circumstances women should study or be taught Torah suggests that women were indeed studying and being taught.[6] Jewish feminist historian Tal Ilan argues that women were members, not just supporters, of the Pharisaic movement, and that they participated in the activities of the Pharisaic table-fellowships.[7]

The Christian Testament evidence about Mary and the women with Jesus can be read in the context of the *basileia* movement. Luke 8:1–3 is a clear statement of women's presence but it is also unclear as to the nature of their participation. While the women's "service" may have originally indicated a powerful leadership position, it can too easily be read as casting them in the roles of financial supporters or servants caring for the physical needs of the men, confining them to private rather than public roles. The conventional view that Jesus surrounded himself with twelve men, and the restriction of the term "disciple" to men in the Gospels further restricts the readers' view of women. Luke-Acts often depicts women as subordinate, passive, and silent. The Gospel of Matthew opens with the story of an endangered woman, Mary, whose story is told, however, from the perspective of interest in the decision of Joseph. Matthew's focus on Peter and the final commission of the eleven in Galilee leaves no room for women.

But they were there. There is evidence that there were married women and mothers in the movement as well as women not identified by such ties (single, divorced, or widowed). Stories of the Syro-Phoenician woman in Mark 7 and the Samaritan woman of John 4 indicate that women were central figures in the *basileia* movement outreach to Gentiles. In the Gospels, both women and men are healed, and Jesus' parables and sayings talk about the experience and daily work of both men and women. Some of Jesus' sayings are directly anti-patriarchal: for example, Jesus commands that his disciples not call anyone on earth "father" (Matthew 23:8) and he calls them to a different kind of family (Mark 3:3 5). Jesus speaks of the divine "Sophia" (or God's wisdom personified as female) as well as "Father." He understood himself and his companions and predecessors as sent by Sophia (Luke 7:35; 11:49; 13:34; Matthew 11:28–39).

Perhaps one can even go further. Mary Rose D'Angelo sees the movement connected with Jesus as one of shared prophecy, based in the collective experiences and communal teaching of co-workers, rather than based only in Jesus' teaching.[8] Others besides Jesus had powers of exorcism and healing. The members may have thought of themselves as wisdom teachers, prophets of Sophia-God reaching out to the oppressed and willing to pay the price for that lifework, suffering as her representatives (Luke 11:49). In such a reconstruction, the teachings of the movement were not about Jesus but about the *basileia* of God. This *basileia* was experienced in the context of common meals, healing events, and religious reflection of the community.[9] In this view, Jesus himself is reconceived as a man who could learn from and with women (Matthew 15:21–28).

If one begins with the view of egalitarianism in the *basileia* movement, then one can assume that whatever the male disciples heard and learned during the ministry was heard and learned by the women as well. This means being open to the idea of the mutual participation of its members. Jesus and others can be seen as resisting the authoritarian dynamic associated with a charismatic leader whose followers would be dependent, and even helpless without him.

In such a movement, a person like Mary Magdalene could be seen as a contributor, partner, and leader, not simply a follower. She may have been Jesus' companion, or his elder, perhaps his teacher or predecessor, in a relationship that may or may not have been sexual. She may also have been his successor.

Our gradually increasing knowledge of Jewish women's lives and options indicates the vitality in some circles of the egalitarian impulse within Judaism, based on the covenantal tradition of Israel. Can more be said about the source and motivation of the egalitarianism of this *basileia* movement of Jesus and his companions? Some scholars imagine that egalitarianism springs from the common struggles of peasant life or extreme poverty. Others locate ancient egalitarian ethics and inclusive meal practice within some kind of progressive Judaism influenced by the larger Greek and Roman culture.

We can be more precise than this. Egalitarianism is a common and constant characteristic of apocalyptic movements throughout history. Many people associate apocalyptic thinking only with end-of-the-world speculation, but such movements often promote egalitarianism and are motivated by the desire for it. Alan Segal writes, "People who join apocalyptic groups feel deprived of something meaningful or valuable to the society but unavailable to all people equally."[10] Future hope and present experience, contemplation, and action are bound up together. If we experience liberation from the fear of personal loss and death, then there is also liberation to pursue a life of righteousness or justice. In my view, familiarity with the prophetic and apocalyptic traditions of the Hebrew Bible, gained in the ordinary course of Jewish life and synagogue attendance, along with intelligent, creative application of these traditions energized the mostly peasant *basileia* movement. The context of oppression in

Roman times united people, peasants and intellectuals, and a living experience of an alternative *basileia* made apocalyptic thinking relevant to people's daily lives. Apocalyptic ideas like the *basileia* of God, the resurrection of the dead, and the vindication of the suffering righteous inspired people to imagine the world in a way that makes those visions of justice a reality. As in the apocalyptic outlook of the book of Daniel, there was an insistence on taking a stand in hope of and faith in final justice. Like others throughout history, Jesus lived this vision of God's justice and was crucified for it.

The Crucifixion and Burial of Jesus

Yet, the women did not flee. Mary Magdalene is named prominently among the women who watch the crucifixion of Jesus in Mark 15:40–41, Matthew 27:55–56, and John 19:25. A group of women watch the crucifixion in Luke 23:49. These same women witness the place of Jesus' burial in Mark 15:47, Matthew 27:61, and Luke 23:55. In John 20:1, it is clear that Mary Magdalene knows of the location of the tomb of Jesus, although the text has not said how she knows.

Are the stories about the women at the cross and the burial of Jesus historical? Some scholars say no, because Rome would not allow sympathizers or relatives at executions. Also, the idea that the body of Jesus would have been given a dignified burial, or any burial at all, has been questioned, since the bodies of the crucified were often left on the cross to be eaten by birds and dogs or wild beasts, or thrown into a common grave or lime pit, or buried in an unknown place. The fact that Mary Magdalene and the other women play no part in the story of the burial is taken by some as further evidence of their absence at the cross. Joseph of Arimathea is sometimes regarded as a fictional character, invented so that an incomplete burial of Jesus by enemies could be changed into a complete entombment by friends.[11]

Scholars often question the historicity of Mark 15:40 (and the parallels in Matthew 27:55 and Luke 23:49) because the phrase "from a distance" resembles a phrase from Psalms 38:11: "My friends and companions stand aloof from my affliction, and my neighbors stand far off." The Gospels are full of such allusions to Jewish scripture, which suggests to historians that the Gospels are creative interpretations of scripture and not eyewitness reports. However, it is also possible that the Gospel writers were interpreting a historical event in light of their scriptures. Perhaps the women stood at a distance because they were not allowed to come close. They are not "aloof" as in the psalm. Nor are they "shunning" Jesus. The distance is a realistic feature of a political execution. This kind of state terrorism was intended to have a significant effect on spectators, especially on the companions of the crucified.

It is historically likely that in spite of the danger to themselves, some women—most prominently Mary Magdalene—*were* present at the crucifixion. The Roman historians Tacitus and Suetonius tell us that when rebels were punished, Rome thought it wise to keep an eye on their sympathizers, friends and relatives, even women and children.[12] The Jewish writers Josephus and Philo report Roman and Jewish arrests of women and even their crucifixions.[13] The Roman governor Pliny, in his correspondence with Trajan, writes of women and men accused and attacked for being Christians in Bithynia, mentioning his torture of two female slaves "who are called deacons."[14] Thus the women, by witnessing the crucifixion, and burial, and then returning to the tomb, were putting themselves at significant risk by admitting their loyalty to this condemned criminal. If one thinks of this *basileia* movement as totally focused around the work of one man and his male followers, then the women's presence

is motivated by their love of Jesus. But if the movement was egalitarian, then the women would have been strongly committed to a vision of the *basileia* that included taking a risk to stand by their
persecuted friend.

In terms of evidence, the case is strong for claiming the historicity of the women at the crucifixion. Although Matthew and Luke
are getting their information from Mark, the Gospel of John is not.
John's list and ordering of names (Jesus' mother's sister, Mary of
Clopas, and Mary Magdalene) is not borrowed from Mark's (Mary
Magdalene, Mary the mother of James the younger and of Joses, and
Salome). Thus the fact that both Mark and John show the women
witnessing the crucifixion suggests that there was an early story of
their presence at the cross that both writers knew independently.
Historical Jesus scholars give weight to multiple and independent
evidence regarding Jesus: the same weight should be given to the
material related to women at the cross and tomb.

There are further historical questions. Was the women's witness
only to the brute fact of Jesus' crucifixion or was it also to some
details? I think it is reasonable to assume it was also to some details,
in particular Jesus' cry from the cross and its misinterpretation as a
call to Elijah. In both Mark and Matthew the dying Jesus utters a
cry in Aramaic or a strange combination of Hebrew and Aramaic:
"Eloi, Eloi, lama sabachthani" (Mark 15:34) or "Eli, Eli, lema sabachthani?" (Matt 27:46). This is a quotation of Psalm 22:1, "My
God, my God, why have you forsaken me?" The cry is misunderstood by some of the bystanders as a cry to Elijah. In Mark, someone
runs, fills a sponge with a vinegary wine, puts it on a reed, and gives
it to Jesus to drink, saying, "Wait, let us see whether Elijah will
come to take him down" (15:36).

The confusion between Eloi/Eli and Elijah is understandable
given that this is a death scene: the garbled speech of one suffocat-

ing is heard in terms of a popular expectation that Elijah will help the oppressed, and will return before "the day of the Lord . . . the great and terrible day" (Mal 3:23; 4:5). More specifically, there is a tradition in a Jewish wisdom text that suggests that Elijah comes to the dying righteous one: "Blessed is he who shall have seen you [Elijah] before he dies" (Sirach 48:11).

But why would they give him a bitter drink? Perhaps the writer is thinking about the text in Psalm 69:21, "They gave me poison for food, and for my thirst they gave me vinegar to drink." But it is not clear why a mention of Elijah would lead to the offering of vinegar. It seems to me that two traditions—one about Elijah and one about the vinegar—have been awkwardly combined by Mark. We know the story about vinegar was circulating around because both Luke and John have it (Luke 23:36 and John 19:29). However, the vinegar is not linked to a cry from the cross in either Luke or John. In John 16:32 Jesus says that even after the disciples flee, God will not abandon him. This may be evidence that the Gospel writer knew the story about the cry of forsakenness on the cross, and rejected it.

My suggestion is that the women's witness to the crucifixion may have included the memory that Jesus cried out the words of Psalm 22:1 or similar words, and that they were misunderstood as a cry to Elijah. Two developments later occurred: (1) Psalm 22 was explored to give further theological depth and meaning to normal execution realities like mockery, stripping the crucified, distributing garments, and thirst. All of these elements then appear in the extended passion stories; (2) Elijah traditions, as will be discussed, very early provided a way to believe in and understand the vindication and resurrection of Jesus.

I think it is likely that women also witnessed the burial performed as a religious duty by Joseph of Arimathea, a prominent member of the Sanhedrin (Mark 15:42–47). As noted, the common

Roman practice was to deprive executed criminals of a decent burial and to leave their corpses exposed on the cross for many days to be eaten by birds.[15] It is unlikely that Pilate would have turned over the body of Jesus to his followers, friends, or family. But he may have turned the body over to Jewish authorities responsible for observing the command in Deuteronomy 21:22–23 that a person who had been executed and hanged should not be left hanging after sunset; he (or she) should be buried on the same day. Josephus insists four times on Jewish concern for proper burial: of those crucified by Rome, suicides, enemies, and those put to death under Jewish law.[16] Thus it is historically plausible that Joseph of Arimathea (or someone like him), observing Jewish law, gave Jesus the quick, minimal burial of a criminal in a nearby tomb. In other words, the Sanhedrin took custody of Jesus' corpse through a delegate, and laid it in a tomb. Presumably the same was done for the other two crucified with Jesus; but the Gospel writers are not interested in this. In later texts, the Sanhedrin is said to have maintained burial places (not a common pit) for the bodies of those executed to undergo decomposition; a year later the bones would be released to the family for burial in an ossuary.[17] This may have been what happened to the crucified Yehohanan, whose bones were found in an ossuary at the first-century burial place Giv'at ha-Mivtar.

If this is what happened, then it is plausible that after the Sabbath the women returned to the tomb of Jesus at the Sanhedrin burial ground for criminals. It is also reasonable to suppose that women who had been present throughout the execution would stay to witness the burial even if they were not allowed to participate in it. They could also have noted the burial site and returned to it. This would mean that the tradition of crucifixion, burial, and tomb could be a pre-Markan set of stories linked by the witness of women. It seems logical that at least Mary Magdalene witnessed the burial, since she is never depicted as ignorant or confused about the location of the tomb she visits on the third day.

The Empty Tomb

According to all four Gospels, women find the tomb empty (Mark 16:6, Matthew 28:6, Luke 24:3, John 20:1–2). But the empty tomb is widely considered by scholars to be a late addition to the passion story, designed to prove the resurrection was real and physical. Claims to have seen Jesus lend authority to those who were leaders in the movement after Jesus' death. For example, Paul's first letter to the Corinthians gives a long list of people who had visions of the risen Jesus: "For I handed on to you as of first importance what I in turn had received: that Christ died for our sins in accordance with the scriptures, and that he was buried, and that he was raised on the third day in accordance with the scriptures, and that he appeared to Cephas, then to the twelve. Then he appeared to more than five hundred brothers and sisters at one time, most of whom are still alive, though some have died. Then he appeared to James, then to all the apostles. Last of all, as to one untimely born, he appeared also to me" (1 Corinthians 15:3–8). Paul mentions neither the women at the tomb nor an appearance to them.

Did he know the stories about the women finding the tomb empty? Paul's statement that Jesus "was raised on the third day" implies that he knows a story about some discovery or revelation or insight on a particular day. Perhaps Paul knew about women and an empty tomb or something like it. If he did, he may have omitted it for political reasons. The topics discussed in First Corinthians as a whole—like marriage, prophecy, celibacy, and women's speaking—suggest there were conflicts regarding women in the Corinthian assembly, disputes over status and authority. Paul does not stand by these women in support of their prophetic speech. It is possible, given what we know of later debates among the gnostics that pit Peter against Mary Magdalene, that the women of Corinth claimed their authority based on the experience of women in the Galilean and Judean *basileia* movement, in particular the women at the tomb. Paul, then, prefers to bolster the authority of Peter and James who were honored as leaders in Jerusalem. First Corinthians 15:1–8 is one of six texts in which *either* Peter or Mary Magdalene receives an individual resurrection appearance. The Gospel of Luke, the Gospel of Peter, and 1 Corinthians 15 are texts about Peter; the Gospels of Matthew, John, and the later version of Mark are Magdalene texts. This suggests that the tension between Peter's authority and Mary's present in the gnostic texts existed already early in the first century.

If there were competing traditions—the women at the empty tomb and the men's visions—then one can ask which came first. Was it the empty tomb or the resurrection appearances? Which one was the beginning of the Christian belief that "he has been raised?" Did people claim that Jesus had been raised because they had visions of Jesus or because the tomb was empty? The appearances to men are regarded by many biblical scholars as the foundation of the resurrection faith. In this view, the women are witnesses to an empty tomb but they do not know what to make of it until the Easter appearances to men explain it; this explanation is then folded into the story of their discovery of the empty tomb by being put on the lips of the Markan young man in white. But this view overlooks a significant question. There are many reports of visions of other dead persons in this period—for example, the visions of Moses and Elijah in the Gospel transfiguration stories. These did not result in the belief that they had been resurrected. Why would these visions of Jesus have such an effect? Is it the visions of Jesus that trigger the Easter faith or is it the empty tomb? Visions are rooted in our experiences and expectations, in hopes and needs. What experiences led to the critical and mystical insight that Jesus had been raised? And why is there such strong evidence of the women's witness at the empty tomb? Why wouldn't the Gospel writers have the men discover the empty tomb if they were also the ones who had the first visions?

Assume for a moment that the resurrection appearances did come first. What did that imply about the fate of Jesus' body? This is difficult to answer. For some people, the absence of the body might be required in order for one to speak of resurrection; for others, not. Such beliefs might have been compatible with a decaying corpse. Alternatively, belief in the resurrection of Jesus might have led to the belief that the tomb was empty (and the invention of such stories). For Paul, resurrection is bodily, but the body that is resurrected is a spiritual body (1 Cor 15:35–44). This could mean that the physical body is left behind in the tomb. Josephus says that the Pharisees believed that "the soul of the good . . . passes into another body."[18] This could also mean that the original body is left behind. Like today, ancient people probably had all kinds of ideas about what happened to the body after death—an absent body might have fit with one of them. But then one must ask again, why the stories about the women finding the tomb empty? The way the Gospels tell these stories implies that the women's presence at the tomb caused some embarrassment and needed some revision. How can we explain the tendency to pass on these stories about women at the empty tomb if the resurrection appearances to men came first?

One could try turning things around and ask what kinds of mystical insights might be inspired by the shock of an empty tomb. What might the absence of Jesus' tortured body imply to someone who was trained in this *basileia* movement, and had witnessed a brutal execution? Drawing on texts like 2 Maccabees, people might have believed that the bodies of martyrs that were destroyed would be restored by God. In Daniel, God raises the righteous dead because they suffer for God's sake; in 1 Enoch because they suffer unjustly. Resurrection speaks to the problem of suffering, injustice, and oppression, and to the human longing to overcome the reality of death. In the Testament of Benjamin, all people are resurrected, not only the persecuted righteous. In 4 Maccabees, immortality and eternal life begin at death; in the Wisdom of Solomon, God makes the righteous immortal already in their earthly life. In texts like 2 Baruch and 4 Ezra, people are resurrected for individual judgment, reward, and punishment.

All these ideas about vindication, resurrection, and life after death may be evoked by the absence of a body. This does not mean that the resurrection must be thought of as the resuscitation of a corpse. Rather, resurrection is compatible with a lost, stolen, or destroyed corpse, or with the idea of ascent to the heavens, or the mystery of the unknown fate of the body. The fact that Paul discusses the nature of bodily resurrection in 1 Corinthians 15 or that Gospel stories depict the resurrected Jesus eating fish, traveling through walls, or inviting disciples to touch him indicates that there was much early Christian speculation about the nature of Jesus' resurrected body. By taking a risk and suggesting that the discovery of an empty tomb by women is a historical memory, one can explain several things: (1) the need to assert that Jesus appeared to his male disciples or to write them into the tomb stories (as in John 20:2–10); (2) the attempts to explain the absence of Jesus' body in light of the scriptures about the vindication of the suffering ones; and (3) the wide variety of materials about the nature of his resurrected body.

Here's my view: the *basileia* movement of Jesus and his companions was apocalyptic. It was egalitarian in some sense, and its combined study, prayer, and actions of resistance were the intellectual and spiritual preparation for the resurrection faith of women who found the tomb empty. No standard, clear expectation of resurrection or vindication was available to them in which to process this emptiness; only an apocalyptic belief in God's victory over unjust suffering through resurrection or exaltation could give meaning to what they had found.

Most historians leave it at this: that the presence of the women at crucifixion, burial, and empty tomb *might be* historical memory. I still have a question. Did the ambiguous emptiness remain ambiguous to the women until it was clarified by the claims of male disciples to have seen the risen Jesus? Or did the women themselves first make the interpretive leap of faith and claim that "he has been raised" (Mark 16:6)? The past tense of this expression—he has been raised—is jolting. In an apocalyptic movement, one might expect the future tense as in Daniel 12:2–3: "your people shall be delivered . . . many of those who sleep in a land of dust shall awake . . . those who are wise shall shine," or in John 11:24 where Martha knows that her brother Lazarus "will rise again in the resurrection on the last day." But let me suggest that the traumatic grief of the women, rooted in a belief that injustice had been done to Jesus and in a confidence in the ultimate, end-time justice of God, produces this theological leap, and the claim that resurrection had taken place.

This means that the emptiness of the tomb rather than the resurrection appearances was the trigger of the resurrection faith, the inspiration of that faith. This does not reduce the resurrection to the women's spiritual experience, rather, it is their physical and intellectual experience that leads them to the spiritual insight that something had happened to Jesus. They were ready to believe it. In the context of the *basileia* movement, scriptures like Daniel 7 and 12 and stories about the ascension of Elijah to heaven were valuable for thinking about the current struggles against injustice. The people of the *basileia* movement—like many movements for change— longed for an end to unjust suffering. The emptiness of the tomb profoundly evokes hope and even faith that God has finally begun to vindicate the suffering righteous.

Apocalyptic and prophetic texts were crucial for the creative and mystical reflection of the movement. There are echoes of Daniel 7 and 12 throughout the Gospels. Many early Christians interpreted the empty tomb in terms of predictions about the Human One (commonly called the Son of Man) in Daniel 7 and the resurrection of dead martyrs in Daniel 12. In my view, the figure of the Human One was central to the egalitarian imagination and ideals of this *basileia* movement even before the death of Jesus. Jesus may have anticipated his own suffering and vindication in light of his confidence in the ideas about the victory of the Human One in Jewish scriptures. Jesus and the other members of the movement understood the Book of Daniel to refer to their own time and to the near future; they need not have been scribes or professional interpreters of scripture to have known the major characters, basic contents, and details of the text.

My hypothesis is that the integration of study and work and mystical experience in the movement was preparation for the earliest attempts to make sense of the death of Jesus. In particular, very general predictions of the suffering and resurrection of the Human One could have been produced before the death of Jesus, given knowledge of the violent death of John the Baptist, popular expectation of the martyrdom of prophets, and the experience of mounting establishment hostility. These would be simple statements of impending doom and vindication, evoked by and invoking Daniel 7:25 and 12:1–2. People would proclaim that the Human One would be delivered into the hands of enemies, and be raised "after three days." I see this time frame of three days as an interpretation of Daniel's measurement of the final suffering, "a time, two times and half a time" (Dan 12:7). These general predictions about the Human One would then be linked to Jesus as in Luke 24:6, which explicitly connects a prediction of the passion/resurrection of the Human One and the fate of Jesus: "Remember how he told you, while he was still in Galilee, that the Human One must be delivered into the hands of sinful men, and be crucified, and on the third day rise."

However, in keeping with the idea that the *basileia* movement was egalitarian and emphasized communal participation, it is also likely that the notion of the Human One meant more than the person of Jesus alone. It is clear from the Gospels that early Christians did understand Jesus as the Human One. In Daniel 7:13–14, the prophet sees the Human One "coming with the clouds of heaven" and receiving a kingdom that "shall not pass away." In the Gospel of Mark, Jesus speaks of the Human One with the same language of coming on the clouds and reigning (14:62). But in Daniel 7:18, 22, and 27, it is the whole community, "the holy ones of the Most High," who receive the eternal kingdom. And in Daniel 10:13–14 and 12:1, the champion of the people is the angel Michael. Thus in Daniel, the figure of the Human One is both singular and plural, both individual and communal. This human/angelic ideal figure stands for the righteous humanity. The idea of the Human One in Daniel can represent, incorporate, and be about people suffering and being vindicated and transformed in resurrection (12:1–3). In this sense, the idea that Jesus was the Human One who has been vindicated and raised up by God, can produce hope for the righteous community as a whole who can now envision their own vindication and victory over death.

If we look at the structure of Daniel 7, we might be able to say even more about the influence of these apocalyptic texts on early Christian thinking and experience. It is possible that the appearance of the angel to the women in Mark 16:1–8 is presented as a little apocalypse (or a scene of revelation) like Daniel 7 or 4 Ezra 13. The text in Mark can be outlined in this way:

A. There is a situation of suffering and grief (the crucifixion and death of Jesus).
B. Something strange is seen: a stone rolled back, a "young man" in white inside the tomb in place of the expected corpse.
C. The women react with amazement.
D. An explanation (Jesus has been raised) is given by the young man, an angelic interpreter.
E. The women are commissioned to tell the disciples of Jesus about a future reunion.
F. The women respond with fear and silence.

Compare this to the structure of Daniel 7:

A. There is a situation of suffering and grief (the oppression of Israel by Antiochus Epiphanes IV).
B. Strange things are seen: visions of four beasts, of the Ancient of Days sitting in judgment, of destruction of the fourth beast, of the Human One receiving authority (vv. 2–14).
C. Daniel reacts: his spirit was troubled, visions terrified him, and he asked an attendant about the truth of all this (vv. 15–16a).
D. An angelic interpretation is given (vv. 16b–18).
B2. Second request and second vision: of fourth beast warring with the holy ones, Ancient of Days judging for them, their reception of the kingdom (vv. 19–22).
D2. Second angelic interpretation is given (vv. 23–27).

F. Daniel's response is terror, silence (v. 28: "As for me, Daniel, my thought greatly terrified me, and my face turned pale; but I kept the matter in my mind"). In Daniel 12:9, Daniel is told by "the man clothed in linen" to go his way, "for the words are to remain secret and sealed until the time of the end."

In Mark 16:1–8, the women receive spiritual insight from a heavenly being and they are commissioned to tell the disciples, but they are silent and afraid. Daniel's silence also signifies that he is overwhelmed and must ponder what he has learned (7:28). Unlike the women, Daniel is told not to tell. However, in both Mark and Daniel the fact that we are reading the book itself breaks the silence. The reader knows that both the women's knowledge and Daniel's get out. This is how apocalyptic thinking works: you talk as if you have the secrets about reality or the future, but they are not really secrets since the secrets are told and reinterpreted again and again. If Mark 16:1–8 is a kind of creative re-telling of Daniel 7, then this is more evidence that the empty tomb was remembered as a crucial site of apocalyptic insight about the fate of Jesus and those who follow him. I think that *not finding the body* was the catalyst for a radical modification of the Daniel tradition, with resurrection understood as ascension like Elijah's in 2 Kings 2. As discussed in the next chapter, John 20:7–8, 17 combines resurrection and ascent (or translation) language in its story about Mary at the empty tomb.

What could all this mean? I think that the point of resurrection language, in the context of Jewish apocalypticism, is that the whole, recognizable person will live in some manner by the power of God, the whole person will be vindicated. The suffering and oppression he or she experienced—from civil and religious authorities—as a result of his or her dedication to justice and as a result of God's dedication, will be overturned. The claim that Jesus had been resurrected is about more than—but not less than—one person's passage through death. As the resurrection of the Human One, Jesus' resurrection is also a corporate resurrection. The symbol of the Human One is used consistently by the author of Daniel, the Qumran community, the author of Revelation and other writers, teachers, and prophets as well as Jesus, none of whom advocated violence, and yet none of whom settled for the status quo. All advocated resistance to the unjust world by imagining alternative worlds in which to sustain a different way of living. The empty tomb traditions, as I read them, draw on such symbolism—which is believed to be not *only* symbolism—to express this faith in the resurrection and vindication of the executed Jesus and of all others who live such an alternative way of life.

We should remember what Elisabeth Schüssler Fiorenza has said, that it is still quite "difficult to prove which tradition was primary, that of the 'empty tomb' associated with women or that of the 'visionary experience' authorizing men." But she presses us to claim our power as readers. She suggests that we privilege the women's tradition and its proclamation that Jesus is going before them to Galilee.[19] This is a statement of presence ahead, not of absence. It is about hope, not failure. This is not a tradition that glorifies, justifies, and glamorizes suffering and injustice, or that "proves" the resurrection. Rather it is a statement of faith in the context of a terrible ambiguity, which remains. It is a call to act in spite of that ambiguity.

A Resurrection Appearance to Mary Magdalene

Who can lay claim to the first appearances of the resurrected Jesus? First Corinthians 15 names Peter as the first witness and yet in Matthew, Mark, and Luke, there is no story of Jesus' appearance to Peter. Although Mary receives a vision of Jesus in John 20, Matthew 28, and Mark 16:9, her name is absent from the list of witnesses in

1 Corinthians 15. Are the visionary traditions in the Gospels later developments that try to connect the empty tomb stories with the resurrection appearances?

In the earliest Gospel, there is no appearance to Mary Magdalene, or to anyone at all, in Mark's enigmatic final scene (16:1–8). Scholars have often wondered whether Mark intended to end the Gospel in this way, with the women afraid and silent. The material that follows Mark 16:8 in English Bibles is considered by many scholars to be added to the original ending of Mark at a later date. The oldest manuscripts of Mark end at 16:8. In one late manuscript, Mark ends only with what is now called the "shorter ending" of Mark (16:8b). Some manuscripts add the "longer ending," verses 9–20. Most manuscripts follow Mark 16:8 with the longer ending in verses 9–20. Following the idea that Mark originally ended with 16:8, one can ask why Mark might have ended the Gospel in this way. Many explanations could be given for the women's silence:

- Mark has an anti-Jerusalem bias, and is saying the Jerusalem disciples and Peter never received the message and did not believe in the resurrection,
- Mark is describing all the disciples (men and women) as failures (and thus calling on his reader not to fail),
- Mark is assuring that the Christian belief in the resurrection is not dependent on the testimony of women,
- The silence emphasizes the secret character of the revelation, which ironically still gets out,
- the silence is not meant to be taken literally, but is a typical response to such a profound experience and is only temporary.

The silence would not be so deafening if the women had not been instructed to go and tell the disciples in 16:7. Maybe that was added later. Regardless, the reader knows the story must move and has moved beyond the women's silence.

It is possible that an earlier version of Mark did not end there. Perhaps a later editor omitted a story of Jesus' appearance to the women and their report to the disciples. If early Christian prophets were making all kinds of claims to visions of Jesus, especially if the visionaries in question were women, those claims would be suppressed by ending the Gospel at 16:8 with the silence. There would also be no link between the empty tomb traditions and appearances to the disciples, which then owe nothing to the testimony of women. If the ending of Mark was suppressed, the author may have doubled the negative in verse 8 just to make that point: "they said to no one (*oudeni*) nothing (*ouden*)."

Matthew, John, and perhaps the longer ending of Mark may contain fragments of an original ending to Mark that involved an appearance of the risen Jesus. Examining the stories of the appearance of Jesus to Mary Magdalene in these texts suggests that a tradition of an appearance to her may have been closely connected with the empty tomb stories. If so, such an appearance was not a late creation designed to be a bridge to the appearances to the disciples. Perhaps an original tradition of Jesus' first appearance to Mary Magdalene has been suppressed in Mark.

The simple procedure of comparing the Magdalene appearance stories in Mark, Matthew, and John, distilling the common elements, produces the following. The longer ending of Mark (verses 9–11) agrees with Matthew and John on five points: (1) the risen Jesus appears; (2) the first appearance is to Mary Magdalene; and (3) that appearance is given a specific time: early on the first day of the week; (4) she is said to have gone and told "those who had been with him" (v. 10; they are described, as in the Gospel of Mary, as mourning and weeping), (5) and the location is at or near the tomb.

Looking closely at Matthew 28:9–10 and John 20:1, 11–18, one can see eighteen points of contact. It seems to me that these eighteen points—plus differences between the narratives and inconsistencies within them—indicate a common tradition lay behind both Matthew and John: (1) the risen Jesus appears (2) to Mary Magdalene (3) early on the first day of the week. (4) The encounter takes place in the vicinity of the tomb. (5) Mary Magdalene does not enter the tomb, but looks into it. (6) The emptiness of the tomb is explained as due to theft or removal of the corpse. (7) She receives the first appearance that is narrated. (8) Jesus utters a greeting. (9) He repeats the words of the angel(s). (10) He is recognized. (11) Touching or holding him is mentioned. (12) Mary Magdalene is given a commission to speak Jesus' own words to the disciples, that is, to be the voice of the risen Jesus. (13) The disciples in this commission are referred to as "my brothers," perhaps an allusion to Psalm 22:22. In neither Gospel does this term refer to the Twelve or the Eleven. (14) The commission is fulfilled. (15) There is no verbal response to the women/woman's message on the part of the disciples. (16) The Holy Spirit is mentioned in the following scene. (17) Neither account is followed by a story of Jesus' ascent to the heavens.

And finally, (18) the role of Mary Magdalene is subordinated or obscured. In Matthew this is accomplished by the appearance to and the worldwide commissioning of the Eleven; in John by the insertion of verses 2–10 concerning Simon Peter and the beloved disciple, who is said to be the first to believe. John 21:14 also says that the appearance on the shore of the Sea of Tiberias was "the third time that Jesus had appeared to the disciples after he had risen from the dead." Either Mary Magdalene is not considered a disciple, or her vision is not counted in this number.

All of these commonalities strongly indicate that there was an early story of an appearance of Jesus to Mary and that this story has been suppressed at the end of Mark and undermined by Matthew and John. This reconstruction and the treatment of John 20 that follows in the next chapter accept the possibility that women were the—or a—primary source of the resurrection faith. The second-century pagan authors who were convinced that female initiative was at the center of Christianity were right. Authors like Celsus indirectly confirm women's active and creative witness from the beginning of the faith. Some will judge this proposal too optimistic or too imaginative. I am willing to risk these charges in order to enter the world of early Christians—a world full of apocalyptic mysticism, visions of an alternative *basileia* of God, the communal experience of injustice, suffering, and loss, and the struggle to produce hope for a transformed world.

CHAPTER 5

Mary Magdalene as Successor to Jesus

> She felt him trying to piece together in a laborious
> and elementary fashion fragments of belief, unsol-
> dered and separate, lacking the unity of phrases fash-
> ioned by the old believers. Together they groped in
> this difficult region, where the unfinished, the unful-
> filled, the unwritten, the unreturned, came together
> in their ghostly way and wore the semblance of the
> complete and satisfactory. The future emerged more
> splendid than ever from this construction of the pres-
> ent. Books were to be written, and since books must
> be written in rooms, and rooms must have hangings,
> and outside the windows there must be land, and an
> horizon to that land, and trees perhaps, and a hill,
> they sketched a habitation for themselves.
>
> VIRGINIA WOOLF
> *Night and Day*

THE STORY OF Mary Magdalene at the empty tomb in John
20:1–18 leaps off the page. It evokes emotion and drama and is one
of several lively exchanges between Jesus and women in the Gospel
of John. The reader wonders who will enter the tomb first? Will
Mary recognize Jesus? Why does he tell her not to touch him? Christian Testament scholar C. H. Dodd once said that John 20 has "an

arresting individuality. . . . There is nothing quite like it in the Gospels. Is there anything quite like it in all ancient literature?"[1] As John tells it, Mary comes to the tomb alone and finds the stone rolled away. She runs to tell Peter and "the other disciple." In this Gospel, Mary speaks. Three times she wonders about the empty tomb: "They have taken the Lord out of the tomb, and we do not know where they have laid him."

Mary's first announcement sets off the odd footrace between Peter and the beloved disciple. Although the beloved disciple out-runs Peter, he does not enter the tomb first but rather follows Peter in. This jockeying means that the beloved disciple (a favorite in the Gospel of John) is the first to believe—although it does not say what he believed—but Peter is still the first to enter the tomb and witness its emptiness. They go home and leave Mary at the tomb.

Mary weeps and looks into the tomb only to see two angels in white. She is asked twice why she weeps—once by the angels and once by Jesus, whom she mistakes for the gardener. Mary admits her fear that she does not know where Jesus has gone. Finally, Jesus calls her name and she recognizes that this is not the gardener after all. She calls him *Rabbouni* and apparently clings to him. He says, "Do not hold on to me, because I have not yet ascended to the Father. But go to my brothers and say to them, 'I am ascending to my Father and your Father, to my God and your God.'" Finally, she goes and reports to the disciples: "I have seen the Lord."

John's story has quite a few distinctive elements in comparison with the other Gospels: the race, the weeping, the garden, the mistaken identity, Jesus calling Mary's name, Mary speaking and calling Jesus *Rabbouni*, the talk of ascension, and the command not to touch or hold onto Jesus. These are all particular to John and yet, as discussed in the previous chapter, the story shares significant points of contact with Matthew 28:1–10. If John and Matthew were written independently of each other, then there was a story about an appearance of Jesus to Mary Magdalene that both Matthew and John knew but reshaped and even downplayed. What was the nature of this story? Could some of the distinctive features of John's version derive from this lost appearance narrative?

I think so. For C. H. Dodd there is nothing quite like this story in ancient literature. But I suggest that there *is* something similar in the Elijah-Elisha story in the Hebrew Bible. Both 2 Kings 2 and John 20 are stories about an intense and erotic bond—though perhaps not romantic or sexual one. They are about grief and loss and about empowering, the transformation and sending of the visionary. In 2 Kings 2, Elisha becomes the successor of Elijah, whom he witnesses ascending to the heavens. In John 20, I hear echoes of this prophetic succession story and thus reverberations of an ancient claim that Mary Magdalene was a successor of Jesus. The soundings are faint: Mary is downplayed in John and in the history of interpretation of John. But if one listens carefully, something still might be heard.

John 20 and 2 Kings 2

I detect traces of an early story about Jesus' appearance to Mary and his ascent in John 20. This telling appears to me to have been an imaginative reuse of 2 Kings 2:1–18, Elisha's witnessing of Elijah's ascent. As seen in the previous chapter, the early Christians regularly drew on and adapted the Hebrew Bible to interpret their experiences and to evoke its sacred and mystical meaning throughout the traditions about the passion of Jesus. Apocalyptic texts like Daniel 7 and 12 and the figures of Elijah and the Human One provided key insights into the nature of the times and powerful language and imagery through which to express those insights. I suggest that something similar may have happened with the story of Elijah's ascent.

In the Greco-Roman world of the time of Jesus, it was commonly believed that one could ascend into the heavens, after death and before it, in dreams, in visions, and even bodily. The Christian Testament is clear that early Christians believed Jesus had ascended after his death and that they expected to do the same themselves. This idea of heavenly ascent was linked to mystical preparations and practices. The goal of the mystic was to come into the presence of God. The claim to have *witnessed* an ascent is powerful stuff biblically, particularly in the mystical tradition. Elisha's witnessing of Elijah's ascent is the sign that what Elisha has asked his master—to inherit a double share of his spirit—will be granted him by God. "Elijah said to Elisha, 'Tell me what I may do for you before I am taken from you.' Elisha said, 'Please let me inherit a double share of your spirit.' He responded, 'You have asked a hard thing; yet, if you see me as I am being taken from you, it will be granted you; if not, it will not'" (2 Kings 2:9–10). With the creative reuse of this text, Mary Magdalene's claim to have seen the risen Jesus ascending may have carried with it the claim to have inherited a double portion of the spirit that was in him. It may not be an accident that in John's re-telling Jesus gives his spirit directly to the male disciples after Mary's announcement.

What leads me to turn to 2 Kings 2 when reading John 20 is the risen Jesus' statement that he has not yet ascended (verse 17), that Mary Magdalene is to tell his "brothers" that she saw him, and especially that he says to her, "I am ascending." This phrase makes the link for me. Elijah tells Elisha that he will ascend and then is witnessed doing so. A chariot of fire and horses of fire separates the two of them, and Elijah ascends in a whirlwind into heaven. Elisha keeps watching and crying out, "My father, my father! The chariot of Israel and its horsemen!" But when he can no longer see him, he grasps his own clothes and tears them in two pieces. He picks up the mantle of Elijah that has fallen from him, then goes back and stands on the bank of the Jordan. He takes Elijah's mantle and strikes the water, saying, "Where is the Lord, the God of Elijah?" When he has struck the water, the water is parted, and Elisha goes over. When the company of the prophets at Jericho see him from a distance, they declare, "The spirit of Elijah rests on Elisha." They come to meet him and bow to the ground before him (2 Kings 2:11–15).

If 2 Kings 2 is behind or within John 20, then several of its elements can be explained. For example, it can make sense of the strangely low christology of Mary Magdalene's address to Jesus as *Rabbouni*, meaning "my dear rabbi" or "my little rabbi." The company of prophets warns Elisha twice, "Do you know that today the Lord will take your master [*adoneika*] away from you?" The terms *rabbouni* and *adoneika* seem roughly equivalent here. In a later rabbinic translation of Elisha's cry, "my father" is changed into "my rabbi." Elisha is a pupil, fellow-prophet, companion, and follower of Elijah; Mary Magdalene is a pupil, fellow-prophet, companion, and follower of Jesus.

If 2 Kings 2 is being alluded to here, then the statement that Mary should not "hold" or "cling to" Jesus may echo the fact that Elisha also refuses to leave his master, as they travel from Gilgal to the Jordan, where Elijah will be taken. Three times Elijah says "Elisha, stay here, for the Lord has sent me." Three times Elisha responds, "As the Lord lives, and as you yourself live, I will not forsake you." And three times Mary Magdalene inquires about the whereabouts of Jesus. The sons of prophets engage Elisha twice prior to Elijah's ascent, and twice Mary Magdalene engages or is engaged by others (disciples, angels) about her search for Jesus.

Both texts have the theme of seeking. In John 20:15, Jesus asks Mary, "whom do you seek?" Mary has been successful in her search for Jesus. In 2 Kings 2:16–18, fifty men seek for Elijah for three days but do not find him. Elisha knows their seeking is useless. In both texts there is only one witness to the ascension who is then sent to others to speak for the one ascended.

In John 20:17, Jesus speaks of "my father and your father" and designates the disciples his "brothers." Also using family language in a spiritual sense, Elisha cries out "my father, my father" to Elijah, and the band is called "sons of the prophets." These are expressions of equal privilege in the family of God, and are part of the Jewish mystical tradition's notion of the transformed mystic and angels in a "celestial family" (3 Enoch 12:5). They echo the communal mysticism of Qumran. In the Gospel of John, mystical union is with the Human One whose ascent allows the community to share the same relationship with God. Jesus does not award the disciples a new status but rather reminds them of the destination they share with him: "I am going to my Father and your Father."

In 2 Kings 2:1–18, Elisha becomes the legitimate inheritor of the spirit of Elijah and the one in whom Elijah's own three-part anointing commission in 1 Kings 19:15–16 will be accomplished. There is no account of Jesus anointing Mary Magdalene, or of Jesus commissioning her by throwing his mantle over her as Elijah does to Elisha in 19:19–21. In the canonical Gospels she is not said to replace Jesus or fulfill his mission. Her following him to his death may in some way be seen as equivalent to crossing the Jordan with him. But there is no evidence that crossing the Jordan was at that time a metaphor for death. Mary Magdalene receives no mantle of the ascending Jesus; she performs no feat like the parting the waters of the Jordan to demonstrate her empowerment. Elisha's empowering is explicit and acknowledged; Mary Magdalene's is not. In fact, there is no response at all to her report, and the spirit of Jesus is said in the subsequent scene to have been breathed by him not on her, but on the disciples.

Did Elijah Die?

It might be immediately objected that the taking of Elijah, unlike the story of the empty tomb and appearance, is not about death or resurrection, but about escaping death. Yet even in the Hebrew Bible and its Greek translation (called the Septuagint), Elijah's ascension may be understood as a death. In 1 Kings 19 the verb *lqh* is used three times. Because his enemies are seeking his life "to take it away" (verses 10, 14), Elijah asks that he might die: "It is enough; now, O Yhwh, take away my life" (verse 4). After Elijah ascends in 2:11, Elisha tears his clothing into two pieces, a sign of mourning. The persecuted prophet is now removed beyond his enemies' reach. Like Jesus' death and resurrection, Elijah's ascension provides him with a new kind of bodily life, beyond time and decay, available for return, recognizable. The cry "My father, my father! The chariot of Israel and its horsemen!" is also repeated by the weeping King Joash before the dying Elisha (2 Kings 13:14). In later Jewish tradition, this cry is repeated in the context of funerals by Rabbi Akiba for Rabbi Eliezer and by Joshua ben Hananiah for Rabbi Eliezer. Rabbi Abahu compares the "taking" of Enoch and Elijah to God "taking" away from Ezekiel the desire of his eyes, that is, to the death of his wife.[2]

Chariot imagery is also used to speak of death in the Apocalypse of Moses 33:34. Eve sees Adam's soul taken "in a chariot of light" borne by four bright eagles, with angels going before it. The death chariot appears also in the Testament of Abraham 14, again with the soul separated from the body: "And chariots of the Lord God came and took his soul into the heavens. . . . And Isaac buried his father Abraham near his mother." Enoch's final translation comes by chariot: "He was raised aloft on the chariots of the spirit and his name vanished among them" (1 Enoch 70:2).

Elijah comes to be associated with resurrection, perhaps because he revives the widow's son in 1 Kings 17. In Ben Sira 48:11, he is linked to the resurrection at the end time: "Blessed is he who sees you before he dies, for you give life and he will live." Mark 9:10–11 is another early witness to this association between Elijah and resurrection, this time of the Human One: "Why do the scribes say that Elijah must come first?"—before, that is, the Human One's "rising from the dead." If Elijah is one of the two witnesses mentioned in Revelation 11:3, then there he is said to be murdered. His body lies unburied for three and a half days, after which he is resurrected and ascends on a cloud (Rev 11:7–11). In the Coptic Apocalypse of Elijah 4:7–19, Enoch and Elijah return to earth, fight the shameless one, are killed, rise up, "lay down the flesh for the spirit," and "will shout up to heaven as they shine." By the time of John the Baptist and Jesus, it was quite possible to think about the violent and unjust death of righteous people and the possibility of resurrection in light of the traditions of the prophet Elijah.

This tradition echoes in the Negro Spiritual "Swing Low, Sweet Chariot," which understands 2 Kings 2 in terms of death and as a story of resistance and liberation. As early members of the *basileia* movement drew on the stories of the death and ascension of Elijah to make sense of their struggles and their hope for vindication, so "Swing Low, Sweet Chariot," was beloved by Harriet Tubman, and sung by her friends the evening she died, March 10, 1913.[3]

A Woman as Visionary, as Successor?

Another objection to my claim that 2 Kings 2 is evoked in John 20 might be that the very idea of a woman visionary, or a woman inheriting the mantle of spiritual authority was unthinkable in the Judaism or Jewish Christianity of the period. There are no examples of female characters ascending to the heavens in the literature of this period; mysticism seems to be a male thing. Access to the most holy places was limited to men.

Still, women's participation in spiritual thought and ritual can be found. Although women may not have functioned as priests in the Jerusalem Temple, they were allowed in every area of the Temple precincts in which men were allowed, passing through the Israelites' Court to offer sacrifices at the altar in the Priests' Court. In the Court of the Women, men mixed freely with them except during the Water Drawing Ceremony held on the Feast of Tabernacles.[4] Luke 2:36–37 depicts the widowed, ancient prophet Anna living in the Temple. In the Therapeutae's sacred ceremony, involving music and eating the holy food, this group of women and men saw themselves conceptually as spiritual priests within the Temple Sanctuary.[5] In any case, exclusion need not stunt the imagination or the spirit. Women were certainly as capable as non-priestly men of knowing themselves *not* excluded from the holy, and of imagining themselves entering the Holy of Holies.

The Testament of Job is a Jewish work from the time during or before the time of the Christian Testament that presents contact with heaven as a possibility for women, and that values women's prophetic, ecstatic activity and leadership. Chapters 45–53 use chariot imagery to portray a death, and show women, Job's three daughters, witnessing an ascent. Here they are engaging in mystical practice, capable of connection with the divine realm and of inheriting spiritual power. If one strand of thought in early Judaism regarded only men as capable of communication with heaven, another strand, represented by the Testament of Job, regarded both women and men capable.

In the Testament, Job's three daughters ask why they did not receive part of his estate, as their seven brothers did. He tells them, "Do not be troubled, my daughters: I have not forgotten you. I have already designated for you an inheritance better than that of your seven brothers" (Job 46:4). The inheritance here is spiritual, symbolized by cords. The daughters each receive a shimmering, heavenly, multicolored cord from the sash or belt God gave Job with which to "gird up his loins" and by which he was cured (*T. Job* 47:2–9; see Job 38:3; 40:7; 42:4). These cords, Job says, "will lead you into the better world, to live in the heavens" (46:3). Job himself has a throne in this better world: "my kingdom is forever and ever, and its splendor and majesty are in the chariots of the Father" (33:2–9). The daughters will now share in his kingdom, receiving "another heart," ecstatically singing hymns in the language of angels (48:3; 49:2; 50:2).

The cords, or charismatic sashes, give the daughters ecstatic powers of language and vision. They enable the daughters "to see those who are coming for [their father's] soul" (47:11). After three days, Job and his daughters "saw the gleaming chariots which had come for his soul. . . . After these things the one who sat in the great chariot got off and greeted Job as the three daughters and their father himself looked on, though certain others did not see. And taking the soul he flew up, embracing it, and mounted the chariot and set off for the east. But his body, prepared for burial, was borne to the tomb as his three daughters went ahead girded about and singing hymns to God" (52:8–12).

This female visionary tradition is linked with the town of Migdal or Magdala, where, in later Jewish tradition, the daughters of Job are said to have died. The Testament of Job, dated to the first century BCE or CE, may have belonged to an unknown Jewish ecstatic-mystical group in which women played a prominent role because of their ecstatic gifts and spiritual insight. Like Mary's story, however, theirs too is often ignored and buried.

Does Mary Misunderstand?

Another objection to the proposal that John 20 resonates with the commissioning scene in 2 Kings 2 comes from privileging the way that John tells Mary's story. Here interpreters give strong weight to the fact that John appears to demean rather than authorize Mary Magdalene. In contrast to the gnostic Mary, in the Gospel of John she is viewed as the woman who misunderstands, whose knowledge is inadequate. Several aspects of the account are said to illustrate Mary's misunderstanding. (1) Her concern for the body of Jesus and her fear that it is stolen are taken to indicate her ignorance about the resurrection. (2) In contrast to her recognition of the risen Jesus in Matthew 28, in John 20 she fails to recognize him, thinking he is the gardener. (3) She calls the risen Jesus *Rabbouni*. The term is a diminutive form of endearment. (The diminutive is particularly interesting: "my little master" undercuts the idea of mastery.) This modest title falls far short of Thomas' "My Lord and my God" in 20:28. Perhaps Mary thinks that Jesus is just like he was before he died. Her use of the title "Lord" in verses 2 and 18 makes this reasoning less plausible, but it is nevertheless a common view among scholars.

(4) Most important is the risen Jesus' command, "Do not touch me" or "Do not go on touching me." The tense of the verb implies that she is already touching him, or is trying to. The verb (*hapto*) may have the notion of grasping or clinging. It could be that the original meaning of the verb, which is mistranslated in John, was "Don't follow me," which would bring us even closer to the story line in 2 Kings 2, where Elisha is following Elijah. The command of the risen Jesus in John 20:17, however, is most often taken in the history of its interpretation as a signal of Mary Magdalene's spiritual

and intellectual inadequacy, her earthiness, her desire to cling to the physical rather than recognizing the spiritual.

Christian Testament scholar Jerome Neyrey reads all of this differently. He concedes the several points in which Mary is painfully not in the know: 20:2 ("we do not know where they have laid him"); 20:13 ("I do not know where they have laid him"); 20:14 (She did not know that it was Jesus); 20:15 ("Supposing him to be the gardener. .ᐟ. . Tell me where you have laid him"). Neyrey sees her transformed, however, into "a disciple supremely 'in the know'" by her recognition of Jesus when he speaks her name. She then provides the disciples with special, mystical knowledge about Christ. For Neyrey, Mary's knowledge of secrets about Jesus (such as where he is going) indicates that she enjoys very high status within the Johannine group.[6] I think this may have been true for some members of the group, but Mary's story is also woven into a narrative in which the focus shifts overwhelmingly to the male disciples. This incorporation results in a distorted stress on her ignorance, not her knowledge.

Although some take this diminished depiction of Mary in John 20 or in the history of its interpretation to mean that John could not have known a positive tradition about Mary, I think this seemingly negative view of Mary confirms the possibility that John is reworking a more positive story about Mary. I have seen this before. In my view, Luke changed Mark's story of the woman who anoints Jesus in a way that marks her as a sinner rather than a prophet. John inserts the story of Peter and the beloved disciple racing to the tomb in a way that demotes Mary from first witness to the resurrection. If one begins with the assumption that Mary's witness was valued by some in the basileia movement, then a negative depiction of her becomes not proof of her misunderstanding but proof of the effort to contain or erase her influence. In the process, however, glimpses of the earlier view of her as successor and visionary are preserved.

Alternative Scriptural Allusions?

Finally, some might object to my proposal that 2 Kings 2 underlies John 20 by suggesting that the Song of Songs provides a more convincing subtext. Both early church writers and modern commentators have seen allusions to the Song of Songs in John 20. The story is set in a garden. A woman seeks an absent man. She holds him and is not willing to let him go. She questions the watchmen. Both texts include motifs of peering, turning, night, spices, arise, touch, and voice. Thinking with this subtext, interpreters have seen John's depiction of Mary as that of "the blind folly, tough-minded devotion, desperate despair, and rapturous joy of the ardent lover."[7] In this context, John 20:17 can be and has been read as focused on the prohibition against her touching him; it is either a rejection of intimacy or a mild chastisement. Since in John's story Mary and Jesus are never together again and never achieve the consummation of their relationship, John 20 overturns the celebration of physical love so apparent in the Song of Songs.

Or perhaps John 20 shows a different kind of consummation. Adela Reinhartz suggests that 20:17 does not reject the physicality of Song of Songs. "Although the beloved is not accessible in the flesh, she has his image in her mind's eye and his words upon his lips." Intimacy, through the experience of Mary Magdalene, is accessible to the reader who acknowledges the subtext; the reader, that is, can see, hear and almost touch the risen Lord through "the signs that are written in this book" (20:30–31). "Whereas on the surface the Beloved Disciple apparently upholds the authority of the disciples as an exclusive group within the community of Jesus' followers, his allusions to the Song of Songs implicitly define Mary as the one who exemplifies the intimacy and love between the believer and the risen Lord."[8]

Granted, Mary's tradition—at least as it is presented in John 20—has become a central site for Christian thinking about bodies, sexuality, the erotic, and physicality, and this may have been true as well in the time of John's Gospel. Mary Rose D'Angelo says that "it cannot be excluded that the danger of a touch between Mary and Jesus involves the sexual connotations of the word 'touch': they are well attested in the period." Although Mary of Bethany is the only character in this Gospel who touches Jesus, other interactions between Jesus and both male and female characters of John also display a "dialectic of erotic and ascetic overtones" and "anxieties about physicality, particularly the physicality of Jesus."[9] It is possible that, in its earlier stages, the community of John contained its anxieties about the flesh by relegating erotic love to the spiritual realm through ascetic practice.

In a male-centered mystical tradition with rigid purity conventions, a woman's touch might be thought of as the touch of someone ritually impure, unable to enter the realm of the sacred. The heavenly body of Jesus might be threatened by uncleanness. But in an egalitarian mystical tradition, concerns about touching or holding would be quite different, and a woman's mystical seeing could be accepted. Mystical texts often contain imagery and poetry that express a desire for God. In the context of such erotic mysticism, Mary Magdalene's desire is not an example of inappropriate knowledge or lack of knowledge, or of how not to behave and think. Rather, her desire is for the relationship that does not break off, for connection with the whole person of Jesus, whatever the cost in terms of anguish. In the context of the apocalyptic and mystical thought world explored here, Mary Magdalene's search is successful. It illustrates the belief that "love is strong as death, passion fierce as the grave" (Song 8:6).

We need not make an either/or choice here: to see John 20 drawing either on the Song of Songs or on 2 Kings 2. The Gospel of John proposes friendship as the bond of the community, and this can be communicated by the use of Song of Songs allusions: "This is my beloved, and this is my friend, O daughters of Jerusalem" (Song 5:16). However, I do not want to emphasize these elements in John 20 to the exclusion of attention to issues of leadership, prophetic visions, and voice. The association of the Song of Songs with Mary Magdalene can make things too easy. It can ease the return to interpreting Mary solely in terms of love. In fact, echoes with the Song of Songs can be so non-threatening to the church that Song of Songs 3:1–4 is a reading used for Mary's feastday Mass in Roman Catholicism. But when love is the only possible interpretation of a woman's relationships, both love and the woman are diminished.

Large Shards

Read in the way I am suggesting, John 20 contains only remnants, large shards of a prophetic succession tradition. Connection with 2 Kings 2 is virtually erased in the appearance to the women in Matthew 28 and to Mary Magdalene in the longer ending of Mark. In this sense, John better preserves the tradition of an appearance to Mary Magdalene. The remnants of a prophetic succession tradition survive in John incorporated, like other aspects of an identification of Jesus with Elijah, into a christology of the descending and ascending Human One. They bear witness to a community that valued the participation and leadership of women. But because they are only remnants, the tradition of empowering Mary Magdalene as successor of Jesus is often difficult to recognize.

It is possible that the material that John used ended with Mary Magdalene's announcement that she had seen the Lord. Jesus does not charge Mary to tell the disciples they will soon see him, as he does to the women in Matthew. In fact, she is just to inform them that he is going. If the text is read on its own, apart from the subsequent scenes with Thomas, Peter, and the beloved disciple, it is clear that they will not see him, and they are to receive Jesus' farewell from her. Mary's role is not a preliminary or transitional one. In any work that may have ended with this scene, Mary Magdalene would be the only guarantor of the vindication of Jesus, and thus of the final message as well. That message implicitly says who she is as his successor, as well as who they are as "brothers." We might imagine the narrative continuing with a series of events consolidating Mary's authority such as the rejoicing of the disciples and the conferring of the holy spirit on Mary and the whole community. But the narrative does not continue in this way.

The Gospel of Luke and its companion the book of Acts preserve an even stronger reaction against the idea of women as successors to Jesus. Luke particularly diminishes Mary Magdalene. In addition, there are many allusions to the stories of Elijah and Elisha in Luke-Acts. Luke is clearly aware of an Elijah christology (9:4; 4:25–26; 7:11–16), and of female prophecy (Anna in Luke 2:36; Acts 2:17 "your sons and daughters shall prophesy"; the daughters of Philip in Acts 21:9). But he makes no link between the two that would empower women. In Luke-Acts, the succession from Jesus to the Twelve is central to the plot. The author draws strong parallels between the career of Jesus in the Gospel and that of the apostles in Acts. Perhaps aware of the necessity of witnessing the ascent for the transfer of the mantle, Luke includes two ascent stories, the first witnessed by "the eleven and their companions" (Luke 24:51) and the second by "the apostles" (Acts 1:9–11). Apart from the recipient of the vision, the ascension scenes in Luke-Acts have a lot in common with John 20:1, 11–18. Is the Magdalene tradition in John a pale and weak imitation of this notion of visionary succession? Or has Luke's appropriation overwhelmed and blotted out a rival? I think the latter. Luke is particularly good at "deal[ing] with the threat of female power by incorporating it."[10]

The empowering of Mary Magdalene was a tradition that apparently did not survive fully and openly in the circles in which the canonical materials were produced. What remain are traces, erasure marks, which lead the readers to wonder what was there in the first place. But the tradition did survive in the circle in which the Gospel of Mary was produced. That gnostic work opens in the time between Jesus' death/resurrection and his departure. After the departure, Mary claims to have had a vision of Jesus, and to have spoken with him about ascent. There is a recognition of that claim and then a rejection of it. Peter knows about the Savior's preference for her, and Levi defends it. Viewing John 20 as a fragmentary glimpse of a prophetic succession narrative about Mary's visions of Jesus' ascent helps us to explain the development of a text like the Gospel of Mary as a counter-tradition to the canonical traditions.

Another gnostic tradition may be reacting in a confused way to John 20 or the source behind it. The Christian writer Epiphanius tells of a lost gnostic story about Elijah and Lilith:

And thus runs their frivolous and fanciful stories, how they even make bold to blaspheme about the holy Elijah, and to claim that a story tells how, when he had been taken up, he was cast back into the world. For, it says, a female demon came and laid hold upon him, and said to him, "Where are you going? For I have children from

you, and you can't go up into heaven and leave your children here."
And he said—so the story goes—"How do you have children from
me? For I was always chaste." The demon says (according to this
book), "But I do! When you were dreaming dreams, you often were
voided by an emission from the body; and I was the one who took
up the seeds from you, and begot you children." Vast is the stupidity
of those who say this sort of thing.[11]

There is no known text or tradition that fits the description of this
exchange, but it might click into place as a possible response to
the Magdalene tradition that I have reconstructed. In this response,
Mary's role as prophetic successor is undermined by association with
sexy, thieving Lilith. Not only did Mary have demons, but when
linked with Lillith she becomes the frightening female demon, in a
weird, one-sided sexual relationship with Elijah/Jesus. Not his companion as in the Gospel of Philip, not the one he loved more than
others as in the Gospel of Mary, but the one who stole his seed.
This tradition may represent both a great hostility toward Elijah
christology and a rejection of Mary Magdalene and all she
represents.

Jesus' appearance to Mary Magdalene was clearly short-circuited
in circles that became dominant in Christianity. It seems that John
or some later editor of the Gospel has incorporated and diluted the
Magdalene tradition. In John 6:62 Jesus asks those complaining
about the difficulty of the teaching regarding eating the flesh and
drinking the blood of the Human One: "Does this offend you? Then
what if you were to see the Human One ascending to where he
was before?" The vision of Jesus' ascension is presented as centrally
important to understanding and accepting Jesus. Mary Magdalene
in the Gospel of John is represented as the believer who sees the
ascending. But the insertion of Peter and the beloved disciple into

the narrative interrupts her story. She is upstaged by the beloved disciple who is the first to come to belief by seeing the grave cloths. The beloved disciple's faith is not dependent on seeing Jesus or on angels. In the Gospel as we have it, the beloved disciple is superior to Mary in faith, and also in authority (21:24). She is upstaged also by the disciples who receive the Spirit from Jesus.

Mary's proclamation, "I have seen the Lord," in John 20:18 is appropriated by the disciples in verse 25. This short form of the resurrection message that does not repeat anything from Jesus' words in verse 17 may replace a more original report, a remnant of which may be found in the second half of verse 18. This verse is an awkward blend of direct speech (focusing on her vision) and indirect (focusing on what the risen Jesus said to her). Now the topics shift. The disciples receive the Holy Spirit and are sent by Jesus to continue his ministry. Thomas learns to prefer belief over seeing. And Peter receives the threefold commission to "feed my lambs" (21:15, 16, 17). At the end of the Gospel, Mary Magdalene fades from view. The scenes in 20:19–21:25 may have been added "precisely to undercut the impression that the definitive interpretation of Jesus' departure was delivered only through a woman."[12]

Still, John's editing and the hearers'/readers' prejudices did not conceal from every hearer or reader the tradition of Mary Magdalene's contribution and empowerment. It is widely held that her importance in gnostic literature and some gnostic circles stems from John 20. Other circles can be imagined that treasured, taught, developed, and acted in response to this story in its ancient or Johannine forms, in different, more inclusive ways. One can read John's depiction of Mary Magdalene in more positive ways. For example, in John the tradition about Mary Magdalene serves as the capstone to a series of stories about women that begins with the mother of Jesus at Cana and includes a missionary, the Samaritan woman, and

Martha, who confesses Jesus as Messiah, the Son of God, and "the coming one." Mary Magdalene then joins the other women in this narrative who come to faith through their own experience.[13] Or, one can read the progression of Mary, to the disciples, to "those who have not seen" (20:29) as a recognition of the availability of the message of resurrection to all people.

The Johannine community was probably independent from other early Christian groups, and may have had a less authoritarian structure. The powerful depictions of women in this Gospel may have been "enabled by the communal prophetic experience that made every believer a source of spirit and life. What little leadership and structure there was seems to have been charismatic and dynamic in character."[14] Mary Magdalene can be seen to stand with Peter and the beloved disciple in a kind of triadic leadership. It is possible that her prominence in John signals the presence of women leaders in the Johannine community at some stage. But her absence from the final scenes in John signals conflicts over such leadership, and may suggest who has won.

Mary's story may have been reshaped in the context of other disputes not specifically about women, such as debates about certain kinds of spirituality and theological ideas. Some scholars suggest that the author was opposed to mystical ascent theology and its belief in the divinization or immortalization of the visionary. Texts that try to limit who can claim to have seen God and God's realm appear frequently in John (see 1:18; 3:13; 5:37; and 6:46). Jesus proclaims that he will not be able to be followed into heaven (at least not before the End). Four times (7:33–34; 8:21; 13:33; 13:36), Jesus tells different audiences that "you will seek me . . . [but] where I am going, you cannot come." If we add John 20:17 ("Do not cling to me") to this list, and read it in the context of seeking to follow (rather than trying to hold back a departure), this verse too may oppose the notion of an ecstatic ascent or visionary experience. The saying might originally have validated more fully the mystical experience of Mary Magdalene as another Elisha who could successfully follow Elijah across the Jordan and return after having a vision. Mary Magdalene's seeing in John 20 would then fulfill in some way the promises of ascension visions to Nathanael in 1:51, and the promises at the supper (14:19, 21; 16:16, 21). The interpretations of John's text, then, which suggest that Mary is ignorantly attempting to hold Jesus back, might miss this possibility. Perhaps, for the Gospel of John, Mary Magdalene understands. But the tradition of her as a visionary must be contained and disguised, diverted.

If an early Christian tradition associated with Mary Magdalene stressed pre-death visionary ascents, some sort of spiritual resurrection, and prophetic empowerment, then these were regarded as incompatible, or only partly compatible, with John's stress on faith. By contrast, in the Gospel of the Savior 107.1–108.64, a vision is a necessary basis for faith and salvation. The risen Jesus' insistence that Mary Magdalene not hold or touch him is echoed, and the reason given: because his glorified body is identified with fire, an image commonly connected to the manifestation of God. All of this suggests that Mary's tradition was alive and rich among the diverse forms of early Christianity. It was apparently significant and powerful enough to be preserved *and* controlled, expanded *and* rejected.

Mary Magdalene Behind the Gospel of John?

I have boldly speculated that a traditional source used in John 20:1, 11–18 emphasized Elijah-Elisha traditions. Scholars have pointed out the allusions to Elijah and Elisha throughout the Gospel of John: the changing of water into wine; healing of the nobleman's son; feeding of the multitude; healing of the man born blind; and perhaps Jesus' prayer at the raising of Lazarus; the expectation of the "coming one." Jesus may have been seen as the eschatological Elijah in a Jewish Christian source used by the author of the Fourth Gospel. In John 1:21 John the Baptist denies he is Elijah, opening the way for an identification of Jesus with Elijah, but this identification never happens in the finished Gospel. The hypothetical source that I have suggested is incorporated into chapter 20 may have been a part of a larger work, which ended with Mary Magdalene's report of her encounter with the risen Jesus or with conflict and (partial) resolution, like the Gospel of Mary.

If Mary was remembered by some as a successor to Jesus, what sort of leadership might have been envisioned for her? Was her "double portion" of the spirit understood to elevate her hierarchically? Or was the spirit understood as available to all in some way through the message? The second option is more probable, since the risen Jesus is *Rabbouni*, not judge or ruler; his God and father is the God and father of all the "brothers and sisters." Mary Magdalene, then, would not be the only successor to Jesus either in this source or in this somewhat egalitarian Gospel, in which all receive the spirit and all will do great works (14:12). John 20:19–31 and 21:1–25 could be appreciated for recognizing and emphasizing this, despite Mary's prophetic role being written out.

But it may be possible to write her back into other sections of the Gospel. An Elijah component in the christology of John's source may have served as a kind of rudimentary Gospel in John's community. Jesus would be understood in this context as an eschatological prophet Elijah, who healed and helped the needy, suffered, and died. In John 1:20–21, John the Baptist denies that he is Elijah. He also denies that he is the Messiah and that he is "the prophet." It is interesting that the first and last of these titles are then given to Jesus. In John 1:41, Andrew goes to Simon Peter and says, "We have found the Messiah." Later in 1:45, Philip goes to Nathanael and says, "We have found him about whom Moses and the prophets wrote." The first and third of the expectations are thus applied to Jesus in John, but the second—Elijah—is not.

There is a similar omission in the sequence of the disciples in 1:35–51. Here two disciples of John the Baptist are presented as the first followers of Jesus; one is Andrew and the other is not named. Andrew then brings his brother Simon Peter to Jesus; the next day Philip is called, and Philip brings Nathanael to Jesus. There is a pattern to the first and third calls:

A. One disciple identifies Jesus to the new recruit (Messiah, 1:41; prophet, 1:45);
B. The disciple brings the recruit to Jesus (1:42, 47);
C. Jesus identifies the new disciple: "You are Simon son of John. You are to be called Cephas" (1:42); "Here is an Israelite in whom there is no deceit" (Nathanael, 1:47).

This pattern is broken in the second call: Jesus himself finds Philip and says to him, "Follow me" (1:43).

These broken patterns and parallels may signal the use of a source which has been edited. Who is the unnamed disciple of John the Baptist? Why is the pattern broken in the second call and what might have stood there originally? And why does an identification of Jesus with Elijah never happen in the finished Gospel? Imagining the reconstructed source, the patterns and parallels can be hypothetically restored. Perhaps there was a threefold chain of disciples recruiting disciples to match John the Baptist's three denials with three affirmations about Jesus. J. Louis Martyn restores the missing disciple recruit this way: "He (Andrew—making a second recruit) found Philip and said to him, 'We have found Elijah who comes to restore all things.' He led Philip to Jesus. And, looking at him, Jesus said, 'Follow me!' "[15]

Let me make a different guess: that in the source, the second unnamed disciple of John the Baptist took the initiative to find Philip, and that disciple was originally a woman, perhaps Mary Magdalene. In this case, the news would pass from Andrew to Simon Peter, from Mary to Philip, and from Philip to Nathanael. This would be a link early in the story between Mary and Jesus-as-Elijah, and make her a companion of both John the Baptist and Jesus. It would represent Mary Magdalene as active and called (1:35–39), and indicate the type of Judaism from which some women members of the movement came. Mention of Mary Magdalene in a source behind John 1 would have introduced her—like the mother of Jesus and the beloved disciple—before the crucifixion. What might have appeared in the source as Jesus' identification of her essential characteristic? As we have seen, gnostic/apocryphal materials identify her as the woman who understood everything, the net-caster, the loved one. This early scene of a call of Mary can be imagined to be related to the tradition of the resurrection appearance to her. A positive response to her report to the disciples is expected there, but missing: their recognition that the spirit of Jesus rests on Mary. Perhaps it was articulated in some segment of the Johannine community, for some time.

The Magdalene Tradition

All this is educated guesswork. But if one can brave angry rejections or the charge of sheer fantasy, there may be more to know about the role of women in apocalyptic and mystical groups. Even if we may not be able to locate its center(s) or its texts, we will be able to imagine more clearly a Magdalene tradition continuing to exist, valued in some communities, building on the basis of wo/men's insight, revelation, and leadership. Seeing this Magdalene tradition as part of the competition among the Peter, James, Thomas, and John traditions, gives a fuller picture of the struggle of and for early Christian egalitarianism. This struggle must be situated in several contexts: (1) within individual ancient Christian communities, and in their different stages; (2) among these communities in their efforts to define orthodox and heretical, inside and outside; and (3) with outsiders like Celsus who ridiculed the resurrection faith as based on the witness of "a hysterical female, as you say, and perhaps some other one of those who were deluded by the same sorcery."[16] The struggle continues today, and has many dimensions.

Whatever else the Magdalene tradition in Christianity may have stood for, at the beginning and in subsequent centuries, the struggle for egalitarianism was central. Community structures and tensions presupposed by the Gospels of Matthew and John and Mary bear witness to this. A vision of the Human One was also central, and imaginations wide, generous, and healthy enough to view this figure as inclusive. Galatians 3:26–28, commonly regarded as an early baptismal formula, may have been in use and understood concretely in terms of social relations. The claim to prophetic succession would have functioned quite differently from the claim to apostolic succession, in that it would have privileged surprise over order. I see Christianity through the lens of the Magdalene as disconcerting, demanding, and deeply vulnerable; and yet, as much as it represented wo/men's empowering speech and sanity, incredibly powerful.

Conclusion

> Now my belief is that this poet who never wrote a
> word and was buried at the crossroads still lives. She
> lives in you and in me, and in many other women
> who are not here tonight, for they are washing up the
> dishes and putting the children to bed. But she lives;
> for great poets do not die; they are continuing pres-
> ences; they need only the opportunity to walk among
> us in the flesh. This opportunity, as I think, it is now
> coming within your power to give her.
>
> VIRGINIA WOOLF
> *A Room with a View*

THE NUMBER OF BOOKS, movies, and TV documentaries on Mary
Magdalene has exploded in the past fifteen years. As in the medieval period, it seems Mary's story is once again a popular place for
thinking about religion, the church, women and men, and the body.
Mary is a cultural icon, whose story continues to change as it meets
different needs, comes under different control, is enacted and mar-
keted and appropriated in different ways. *Every* re-telling of Mary's
story and re-imagining of her image is always part of a much larger
discussion about how the world is and/or what it should be.

For many people, Mary Magdalene has come to stand for wom-
en's agency and vision. Research on Mary Magdalene has created
new understandings of Christian history that inform the ongoing
struggle for equality in church and society. However her legends

also represent women throughout history who have been distorted, ignored, appropriated, and denied authority. Mary's story casts light on the way society stigmatizes wo/men's sexuality and fears wo/men's intelligence.

Too often, there is an obsession with Mary Magdalene's sexuality. Usually it marks Mary as a typical (sexual, sensual, passionate) woman. Sometimes Mary's sexuality helps make Jesus more human. Sometimes it promotes feminine images of the divine and roots female sexuality in the realm of the sacred. I prefer to let lie the issue of the sexuality of Mary Magdalene, in that I let it remain ambiguous whether or not she and Jesus were lovers. Does tolerating ambiguity erase Mary's sexuality? That is not my intent. By looking at the entire Magdalene tradition, I am trying to resist her reduction and fragmentation, to avoid seeing her only as protagonist in a love story, as madwoman, or victim, or lone hero, and also only as religious intellectual and leader. Attempting such resistance is resisting our own fragmentation. Intentionally focusing on the tradition of the women at the tomb and of the appearance to Mary Magdalene warns the imagination not to confine Mary Magdalene to a romantic relation to Jesus, to a personal, private, emotional relationship, whether sexual or spiritual or both. It avoids confining her to any type of relationship with Jesus and tries to see her in her own right. This does not mean she had no sexuality. Rather it presses us to imagine her sexuality as part of her creative wholeness, but not as her whole story. Let us insist on this, for Mary Magdalene as for ourselves.

I believe Mary's and wo/men's creative and spiritual insights were and are crucial elements to Christian faith. I have tried to present convincing, coherent arguments that this is possibly bedrock tradition: that women were at the crucifixion, burial, and tomb. That they found it empty, and that they, or Mary Magdalene alone, received a revelation interpreting that emptiness as resurrection. That Mary Magdalene claimed—or it was claimed by others—that she had a visionary experience of Jesus which empowered her with God's spirit.

Resurrection and ascension, side by side or overlapping, are expressions of belief in the vindication of Jesus and of all those incorporated into the Human One. This insight or revelation about the resurrection of Jesus comes from interpreting Scripture as is recognized in John 20:9 ("for they as yet did not know the Scripture that he must rise from the dead") and in First Corinthians 15:3–4 ("according to the Scriptures"). The stories of the empty tomb and the appearance to the women show that Daniel 7, 12, and 2 Kings 2 were the primary texts that informed the interpretive imagination and produced the Easter faith.

However these stories do not represent a rational explication of Scripture or an attempt to justify claims to visions after the fact. In the case of the empty tomb and the appearance to Mary Magdalene, there is first the jolt of emptiness and then an innovation, a revelation. Apocalyptic and prophetic texts, contemplated beforehand, were re-experienced in intense mourning and waking visions. Such mystical experiences must have been intense and immediate. Mary's revelation of the resurrection and vindication of Jesus comes in the context of the harsh realities of suffering and state torture, and in the real-life struggles against domination. This experience is central; without flesh and bone struggle of life and death, no meaningful belief in resurrection.

The fragments of the claim that Mary Magdalene was a successor of Jesus in John 20 suggest to me that early Christians understood the message of the resurrection of the Human One in continuity with the prophetic and mystical traditions of Israel. The reuse of 2

Kings 2 confirms the existence and efforts of those seeking or continuing change, claiming the prophetic tradition for wo/men. Although this claim was not unique, I understand it as characteristic
of the ideals of the *basileia* movement of Jesus and his companions.
That vision of liberation and egalitarianism at the origins of Christianity is part of its debt to Judaism. The ongoing struggle to realize
that vision in Christianity is evidence that the hierarchical structures of the church too often distort its promise.

Because it is important to tell the story of that struggle, I am not
willing to stop trying to "do" history, to let go of possible evidence
of both historical power and the lack or weakening of power. In my
judgment, historians have not made a reasonable case for the absence of the women at the cross and burial and tomb, or for the
lateness of the claim that Mary Magdalene received a resurrection
appearance. So I have taken my turn with the texts. If I have failed
to present a convincing, comprehensive reading, I hope I have failed
well enough to destabilize existing authoritative readings and the
oppressiveness of the whole Magdalene tradition, to suggest at least
to some readers new ways of thinking, and to encourage the desire
to continue inquiring and trespassing. The deepest knowledge results from dialogue that involves the largest number of differing van-
tage points, all partial, rather than from a singular perception
regarded or regarding itself as authoritative.

And does it really matter, in the end, if all of this is historical or
not? If Mary Magdalene was a fictional, literary character, and these
claims for her legendary, she could still empower and be a resource
for contemporary wo/men. We can read the Gospels any way we
want and need to, as every previous generation has done; we can
seek to grasp what the texts once meant and mean, and to participate in their seemingly inexhaustible capacity to bear many mean-

ings. Our history is not determined by powerful precedents nor by bleakness. Both history and literature can inspire work for social transformation.

Some may find the historical Mary Magdalene or the Mary Magdalene of biblical scholarship boring compared to the flamboyant character of legends and art. I would like to have found a Mary Magdalene as bold and courageous as Virginia Woolf's Ethel Smyth: "She is of the race of pioneers, of pathmakers. She has gone before and felled trees and blasted rocks and built bridges and thus made a way for those who come after her" (from a speech in 1931). But history can most often merely tantalize with such possibilities. I am drawn to what it does provide: only shadows and traces, and the impossibility of knowing with certainty. The Christian Testament's narratives of the empty tomb and of an appearance to Mary Magdalene are in many ways like the site at Migdal. They have been looted, dug at, abandoned, endangered. Many luxury hotels have been built on them. They are a site from which many have been excluded.

But we can climb the fences, walk on it, dig and sift and treat it with respect, even foolishly imagine buying it and owning it. Underneath it lies part of our history. If the tremendous amount of energy expended by Western culture suppressing, remaking, and recovering Mary Magdalene is any indication, then she must have had—and still has—something startling and challenging to say.

Important Terms

Androcentric or androcentrism: A point of view or way of expression that is male-centered. Cultural systems and language that present maleness as normal and femaleness as secondary or peripheral are androcentric.

Apocalyptic: A type of ancient religious writing that features mysterious divine knowledge revealed through heavenly messengers, dreams, and inspired visionaries. The book of Daniel is an example of apocalyptic literature. Also, a religious worldview that looks to God's intervention in history and finds hope in visions of God's justice.

Apocryphal: Ancient Jewish and Christian writings not included in the official canon of scripture.

Ascetic or asceticism: Renouncing human comforts and pleasures and/or claiming one's own religious agency through adoption of disciplines such as fasting, celibacy, and communal or solitary living.

***Basileia* of God:** The kingdom or reign of God was a central feature of the movement of Jesus and his companions and co-workers. The Greek word *basileia* is a political word meaning domain, or imperial rule, or realm. In order to disrupt the tendency to imagine God in the male-centered and politically hierarchical language of human monarchy, I leave the word untranslated. The *basileia* was and is a sacred vision of the way the world would be/might be/could be and thus functions to resist, and envision alternatives to the way the world too often was and is.

BCE: see CE

Canonical and non-canonical: Terms used to distinguish ancient writings that are considered scripture by Jewish and Christian tradition (canonical, in the canon) and those that are not (non-canonical, not in the canon).

CE and BCE: In light of the religious and cultural diversity of Western culture, many scholars now use CE (common era) and BCE (before the common era) in order to recognize and move away from the Christian-defined terms AD and BC.

Christian Testament and Hebrew Bible: These terms for the New and Old Testaments attempt to recognize the religiously diverse nature of the world and remove the evaluative language of "new" and "old."

Egalitarianism: A social vision based on the full participation of all kinds of men and women.

Gnostic: A term traditionally used to describe various Christian heresies. Broadly speaking, gnostic texts or groups can be said to share: 1) an emphasis on knowledge (*gnosis*, in Greek) as a means of salvation, rather than faith or obedience; (2) an emphasis on seeking the truth of one's own divine, inner self, whose true origin and home are somehow beyond the physical or worldly (that is, are transcendent); (3) an emphasis on visionary experience and mystical religious practices that give people insight into the true nature of reality.

Hebrew Bible: see Christian Testament

Kyriarchy: The rule of the Lord and Master (*kyrios* in Greek). A term coined by feminist biblical scholar Elisabeth Schüssler Fiorenza for speaking of complex systems of domination that are characterized by interlocking hierarchies based on sex/gender, race, status/class, age, health, nationality, etc. This term better expresses the complexity of oppressions than patriarchy.

Mysticism: Religious traditions that emphasize union with the divine through meditation, ecstatic experience, or trance-like contemplation.

Sophia: The Greek term for Wisdom. Used in the Hebrew Bible and the Christian Testament as a feminine image of God. See Proverbs 8:1-9:6 and Luke 7:35; 11:49.

Wo/men: A way of writing the word "women" proposed by feminist biblical scholar Elisabeth Schüssler Fiorenza. Writing "wo/men" disrupts expectations and reminds the reader that women are not alike, they differ according to class, race, sexuality, religion, nation, and experience. The slash also indicates that there are marginalized men in the world and throughout history who also face oppression and who struggle for dignity and equality.

Questions and Resources for Discussion

Introduction: Mary Magdalene in the Past and Future
Discussion Questions

1. If we can't know with certainty the historical facts about Mary Magdalene, why is it important to study her story?

2. From what place do you come to this text? What cultural, economic, educational, or religious aspects of your own background influence how you understand Mary Magdalene?

3. What "rubble" might you personally need to sift through in order to learn about Mary Magdalene or yourself?

Resources for Extending Your Study

For additional details and reflections on the study of Mary Magdalene and the feminist insights of Virginia Woolf, see Jane Schaberg, *The Resurrection of Mary Magdalene: Legends, Apocrypha, and the Christian Testament*. New York: Continuum, 2003. Pages 7–46.

See also:

Schüssler Fiorenza, Elisabeth. *Wisdom Ways: Introducing Feminist Biblical Interpretation*. Maryknoll, NY: Orbis, 2001.

Chapter One: A Dig of One's Own
Discussion Questions

1. If you knew a benefactor who could finance an archaeological dig and restoration at Migdal, would you encourage that person to support the project? Why or why not?

2. Why do you suppose written history is so often limited to the stories of important men and wars? What else would you include if you were writing the history of a town and its people?

3. What does it mean to you to say Migdal is our "irresistible decay, our necessary ruin"? In what ways do the Migdal "ruins signal simultaneously an absence and a presence?" What is lost and what is found?

4. What kinds of places and things should we preserve today so that the people of the future will remember wo/men's contribution to religion and society?

Resources for Extending Your Study

For additional details about Migdal, see Jane Schaberg, The Resurrection of Mary Magdalene: Legends, Apocrypha, and the Christian Testament. New York: Continuum, 2003. Pages 47–64.

See also:

Crossan, John Dominic, and Jonathan Reed. Excavating Jesus: Beneath the Stones, Behind the Text. San Francisco: HarperSanFrancisco, 2002.

Meyer, Carol. "Recovering Objects, Re-Visioning Subjects: Archaeology and Feminist Biblical Study." In A Feminist Companion to Reading the Bible. Edited by Athalya Brenner and Carole Fontaine. Sheffield: Sheffield Academic Press, 1997.

Vamoush, Miriam Feinburg. Daily Life at the Time of Jesus. Nashville: Abingdon Press, 2001. (For those interested in using archaeology to imagine wo/men's daily lives, this highly accessible book has a lot of images and drawings).

Website for Biblical Archaeology Review:
http://www.bib-arch.org/bswb_BAR/indexBAR.html

Chapter Two: Thinking Back through the Magdalene

Discussion Questions

1. Were there any surprises for you about Mary Magdalene in this chapter?

2. Why do you think the image of Mary Magdalene as "whore" persists in our culture, despite evidence to the contrary?

3. Compare the anointing women stories in Mark 14:3–9, Matthew 26:6–13, John 12:1–8, and Luke 7:36–50. How are they similar and different in their depiction of the woman, of Jesus, and of the point of the story?

4. How do you feel about the creative use of historical figures in fiction, film, and art? Is it legitimate to use a figure like Mary Magdalene as the basis for creating a new story or work of art that does not correspond with historical fact or with the biblical text?

5. Find a visual image of Mary Magdalene. What ideas does it convey? How?

6. In what sense does the legend of Mary Magdalene become "the story of all women"?

7. Is there any potentially positive effect of the legend of Mary as whore/lunatic/repentant sinner? For whom and in what ways?

8. Is the conflated Mary of legend the only Mary Magdalene you have encountered in your religious or literary experience? Or has some other understanding of Mary found its way to you? If so, how?

9. Would evidence of a sexual relationship between Mary and Jesus influence your view of Jesus' message? Why or why not?

10. If the power of Mary's legends is primarily about "the power of God to redeem. When this great sinner is reconciled to God, we know that no one is beyond the reach of God's mercy," is this empowering or disempowering for wo/men of today? How?

Resources for Extending Your Study

For additional details and reflections, see Jane Schaberg, *The Resurrection of Mary Magdalene: Legends, Apocrypha, and the Christian Testament.* New York: Continuum, 2003. Pages 65–120.

See also:

Haskins, Susan. *Mary Magdalen: Myth and Metaphor.* New York: Harcourt, Brace & Co., 1993.
http://www.catholic-forum.com/SAINTS/golden230.htm (the full text of the Golden Legend)
http://www.earlychristianwritings.com/ (an excellent site for available online resources and translations for all early Christian texts up to 250 CE)
Lahr, Jane. *Searching for Mary Magdalene in Art and Literature.* New York: Welcome Books, 2006.
Mary Magdalene: Intimate Portrait, VHS hosted by Penelope Ann Miller, 1995 (includes a lot of Magdalene art).
Tatum, W. Barnes. *Jesus at the Movies: A Guide to the First Hundred Years.* Revised and expanded edition. Santa Rosa, CA: Polebridge Press, 2004.

Chapter Three: The Woman Who Understood (Too) Completely

Discussion Questions

1. Has your understanding of Mary Magdalene changed from this presentation of her portrayals in the gnostic and apocryphal texts? If so, how? In your view, what is the value of knowing about these texts?

2. How does the profile of Mary in these texts compare with the legends about Mary Magdalene as a repentant prostitute and contemplative discussed in the last chapter? Which one do you prefer or find more powerful and why?

3. In her gnostic profile, Mary Magdalene talks a lot—asking questions, interpreting, comforting, and teaching. She has so much to say that the male disciples complain about it. What do you make of this feature of Mary's profile? In your experience, when does wo/men's speaking become "too much" for a community? How and why do communities try to limit wo/men's speaking?

4. The Gospel of Philip seems to be ambiguous about Mary's relationship with Jesus in a way that calls its readers to "a maturity that gets beyond the false dichotomy of marriage versus celibacy." How do you understand this idea? What might such maturity look like today? How do you think religious people should view the body and sexuality?

5. How do you interpret the figure of Peter in The Gospel of Mary? What is he angry about and why?

6. What do you think of the gnostic emphasis on experiential religious knowledge (through study, seeking, and mystical or spiritual experiences)? How does it compare with your own views on spirituality and those of religious communities that you know?

7. What similarities and differences do you see between the qualities and struggles of the gnostic Mary and wo/men of today?

Resources for Extending Your Study

For additional details and reflections, see Jane Schaberg, *The Resurrection of Mary Magdalene: Legends, Apocrypha, and the Christian Testament*. New York: Continuum, 2003. Pages 121–203.

See also:

http://www.earlychristianwritings.com/ (an excellent site for available online resources and translations for all early Christian texts up to 250 CE)

King, Karen L. The *Gospel of Mary of Magdala: Jesus and the First Woman Apostle*. Santa Clara, CA: Polebridge Press, 2003.

Pagels, Elaine. *Beyond Belief: The Secret Gospel of Thomas*. New York: Random House, 2003.

The Nag Hammadi Library. Rev. Ed. Edited by James M. Robinson. San Francisco: HarperCollins, 1990.

Chapter Four: The Women Did Not Flee

Discussion Questions

1. What do you see differently if you think about the movement of Jesus and his companions as a Jewish *basileia* movement, inspired by apocalyptic visions of

God's realm and by egalitarian ideals? Does it change how you think about Jesus, Mary Magdalene, yourself, and contemporary Christian communities?

2. Choose a story from the Gospels. Re-tell the story from the point of view of a wo/man (a male or female under a situation of domination like patriarchy, poverty, or slavery). What is the message for that person? Can you imagine that person as a central actor in the story? What would s/he do and say?

3. Read Mark 14–16. If you could hear from the woman who anoints Jesus, from the women at the cross, or from Mary Magdalene herself, what would they say to you? What would they say to the writer of Mark? How about to contemporary people facing injustice and suffering?

4. Do you think it is likely that Mary Magdalene had a vision of the risen Jesus at the empty tomb? Why or why not? (Among other things, you might weigh the *absence* of this appearance in the earliest version of Mark and First Corinthians against the *presence* of an appearance in Matthew, John, and the longer ending of Mark).

5. If the presence of the women at the cross and the tomb is historical, then it was also a considerable risk that these women took. When do people take risks on behalf of their beliefs and their hopes for human justice and equality? What happens when people do stand up and take these risks?

6. Does it make any difference to you whether the women or the men in the Gospels are the first to see the risen Christ? Why?

7. What does it mean to say that the empty tomb means presence and not absence? What kinds of experiences remind people that God is with them in the face of tragedy, and that there is life in the midst of death?

8. Mary and other early Christians interpreted the death of Jesus and the empty tomb in light of their scriptures and religious commitments. How does your own worldview and education influence the way that you understand events in your own life and in your community? Give an example.

9. Do you see the Christian Testament texts differently after having studied the gnostic and apocaryphal texts about Mary in chapter 3? How?

Resources for Extending Your Study

For a detailed discussion of Christian Testament scholarship on the texts discussed in this chapter, see Jane Schaberg, *The Resurrection of Mary Magdalene: Legends, Apocrypha, and the Christian Testament*. New York: Continuum, 2003. Pages 204–99.

See also:

Crossan, John Dominic. *Jesus: A Revolutionary Biography*. San Francisco: Harper-SanFrancisco, 1994. While Crossan agrees that the movement around Jesus was inclusive and counter-cultural, he suggests that the empty tomb stories are late and invented.
Kraemer, Ross, and Mary Rose D'Angelo. *Women and Christian Origins*. Oxford: Oxford University Press, 1999.
Schüssler Fiorenza, Elisabeth. *In Memory of Her: A Feminist Theological Reconstruction of Christian Origins*. 10th anniversary ed. New York: Crossroad, 1994.

Chapter Five: Mary Magdalene as Successor to Jesus

Discussion Questions

1. Read Matthew 28:1–10 and John 20:1–18. What are the similarities and differences? How does John's version change the meaning or emphasis of the story?

2. Read 2 Kings 2 and John 20:1–18. Can you imagine that John's story echoes the prophetic succession story of Elisha? How does reading John 20 in light of 2 Kings 2 change your understanding of John?

3. Is it thinkable that Mary Magdalene (and other wo/men) were understood as successors of Jesus and as religious visionaries? Why or why not? What difference does it make?

4. What do you think that Jesus means when he says to Mary "do not touch me" or "do not hold onto me" (John 20:17)? Is she holding him back or straining forward toward her own mystical ascension and union with the divine?

5. What does it mean to say that Mary's "desire is for the relationship that does not break off, for connection with the whole person of Jesus?" How can Mary's connection with Jesus be both physical and spiritual without necessarily being sexual?

6. Does the criticism or suppression of Mary's story still get used today to push certain kinds of religious knowledge and leadership to the margins?

7. In your own society/community, what influences lead toward egalitarian roles and structures? What are the pressures or values that lead to privileging some people over others?

8. How are leaders identified in the various circles you participate in? What might the Magdalene traditions have to say about how leaders are identified, supported, and given authority?

9. Does your study of the Mary Magdalene traditions alter the way that you think about contemporary Christianity? What hopes do you have for the future of society and/or your community in light of your understanding of the past?

Resources for Extending Your Study

For more detail and reflection on John 20, see Jane Schaberg, *The Resurrection of Mary Magdalene: Legends, Apocrypha, and the Christian Testament*. New York: Continuum, 2003. Pages 300–356.

See also:

Hearon, Holly. *The Mary Magdalene Tradition: Witness and Counter-Witness in Early Christian Communities*. Collegeville, MN: Liturgical Press, 2004.
Reinhartz, Adele. *Befriending the Beloved Disciple: A Jewish Reading of the Gospel of John*. New York: Continuum, 2001.

Notes

Introduction: Mary Magdalene in the Past and Future

1. Helmut Koester, "Epilogue," in *The Future of Early Christianity*, ed. Birger A. Pearson (Minneapolis: Fortress, 1991), 475.

2. Neil Gillman, *The Death of Death: Resurrection and Immortality in Jewish Thought* (Woodstock, VT: Jewish Lights, 1997), 30–31.

3. Caroline Walker Bynum, *The Resurrection of the Body in Western Christianity, 200–1336* (New York: Columbia University Press, 1995), 343.

Chapter One: A Dig of One's Own

1. Quoted in Epiphanius, *Panarion* 26, 3, 1.

2. Virginia Woolf, *To the Lighthouse* (Hogarth Press, 1927; London: Routledge, 1994), 33.

3. Strabo, *Geography* XIV, 2, 45.

4. *y. Ta'anit* 4, 69c and *Midrash Ekha* 2, 2, 4.

5. *Pesiqa de Rab Kahanah* [Pisqa 7]; *Wayyikrah Rabbah* 17:4; *Ruth Rabbah* 1:5.

6. *T. Job* 46–52.

7. Josephus, *Jewish War* 2. 598–99.

8. Josephus, *Life* 153.

9. 1 Maccabees 9:2; Josephus, *Antiquities* 12. 420–25.

10. Ibid., 14. 423–26.

11. Josephus, *Life* 30; *Jewish War* 2. 572–76.

12. Ibid., 2. 608.

13. Ibid., 2. 634–38, 641.

14. Josephus, *Life* 463–504.

15. Josephus, *Jewish War* 3. 462–505.

16. Ibid., 3. 532–42

17. James F. Strange, "Some Implications of Archaeology for New Testament Studies," in *What Has Archaeology to Do With Faith?* eds. James H. Charlesworth and Walter P. Weaver (Philadelphia: Trinity Press International, 1992), 42–43.

18. Captain Wilson and Captain Warren, *The Recovery of Jerusalem*, ed. W. Morrison (New York: Appleton, 1871), 299.

19. James F. Strange and Herschel Shanks, "Has the House Where Jesus Stayed in Capernaum Been Found?" *Biblical Archaeological Review* 8 (1982): 26–37.

20. John Wilkinson, *Egeria's Travels* (London: SPCK, 1971), 194.

21. Michael S. Roth with Claire Lyons and Charles Merewether, *Irresistible Decay: Ruins Reclaimed*, foreword by S. Settis (Los Angeles: The Getty Institute for the History of Art and the Humanities, 1997), vii.

22. Ibid., 25.

Chapter Two: Thinking Back through the Magdalene

1. P. Lemos, "Divine Duos," *Ms. Magazine* (Jan/Feb 1989): 126.

2. Quoted in Martin Scorcese, *Scorcese on Scorcese*, eds. D. Thompson and I. Christie (London: Faber and Faber, 1989), 225.

3. Clement, *Paidagogos* 2.8.

4. Origen, *Against Celsus* II.55.

5. Ibid., I.65.

6. Tertullian, *Against Marcion* 4.18.9, 16–17.

7. Tertullian, *Against Praxeas* 25.2.19–21.

8. Irenaeus, *Against Heresies* 5.7.1; 5.31.1.

9. Hippolytus, *Commentary on the Canticle of Canticles* 8.2; 24.60.

10. Jerome, *To Pammachius* 35.

11. Ambrose, *Of the Holy Spirit* 3.11.74.

12. Gregory of Nyssa, *Against Eunomius* 3.10.16.

13. Origen, *Against Celsus* V.62.

14. Gregory the Great, *Homily* 33 on Luke 7 (PL 76, 1239–40).

15. See BHL 5439; printed in *Acta Sanctorum*, July V:218–21; also in PL 133, 713–21.

16. Honorius of Atun, *Speculum Ecclesiae: De Sancta Maria Magdalena*, PL 172, 979.

17. David Mycoff, *A Criticial Edition of the Legend of Mary Magdalene from Caxton's Golden Legend of 1483* (Salzburg: Universität Salzburg, Institut für Anglistik und Amerikanistik, 1985), 2.

18. All quotations in this summary are from Mycoff, *Criticial Edition*.

19. See David Mycoff, *The Life of Saint Mary Magdalene and of Her Sister Saint Martha* (Kalamazoo, MI: Cisterian Publications, 1989).

20. Elisabeth Schüssler Fiorenza, "A Feminist Critical Interpretation for Liberation: Martha and Mary: Luke 10:38–42," *Religion & Intellectual Life* 3 (1986): 21–36.

21. Susan Haskins, *Mary Magdalen: Myth and Metaphor* (New York: Harcourt, Brace & Co., 1993), 328, 364.

22. Katherine Ludwig Jansen, *The Making of the Magdalen: Preaching and Popular Devotion in the Later Middle Ages* (Princeton, NJ: Princeton University Press, 2000), 334–35.

23. John Meier, *A Marginal Jew: Rethinking the Historical Jesus* (New York: Doubleday, 1991), 673 n. 57.

24. Haskins, *Mary Magdalen*, 485–86 n. 42.

25. John Shelby Spong, *Born of a Woman: A Bishop Rethinks the Birth of Jesus* (New York: HarperCollins, 1992), 187–89.

26. Virginia Woolf, *A Room of One's Own* (New York: Harcourt, Brace, & World, 1929), 35–36.

27. Elisabeth Schüssler Fiorenza, *Jesus: Miriam's Child, Sophia's Prophet* (New York: Continuum, 1994), 14.

28. Taslima Nasreen, *Femmes, Manifestez-Vous* (Paris: Des Femmes, 1994), 65–67.

29. A question raised in the National Film Board of Canada's video on the pornography industry, *Not a Love Story* (1981).

30. Anne Hollander, "A Woman of Extremes," *The New Yorker* (October 3, 1994): 113, 117.

Chapter Three: The Woman Who Understood (Too) Completely

1. Sophia of Jesus Christ, III/4,118, 6 and BG 16.

2. Gospel of Philip 74, 13–16; 81, 34–82, 10; 75, 14–25.

3. Dialogue of the Savior 144, 16 and 22.

4. Antti Marjanen, *The Woman Jesus Loved: Mary Magdalene in the Nag Hammadi Library and Related Documents* (Leiden: Brill, 1996), 78–79.

5. First Apocalypse of James, 41, 15–19.

6. Acts of Philip, VIII, 4.

7. First Apocalypse of James, 35, 5–9 and 38, 20–23.

8. Pistis Sophia, III, 113.

9. See ibid., II, 96 and I, 8.

10. The following sections of Pistis Sophia are referred to in this paragraph: I, 17, 5–9; I, 52; I, 60; I, 24, 2; I, 25, 2–3; I, 46, 42–45; III, 113; III, 120; III, 121.

11. Gospel of Philip, 59, 6–10.

12. Pistis Sophia, I, 2–4 and II, 17.

13. Manichaean Psalm Book, II, 187.

14. Dialogue of the Savior, 139, 12–13; 141, 12–14; and 140, 14–18.

15. The following sections of Pistis Sophia are referred to in this paragraph: II, 96; I, 19; I, 34; II, 88; and I, 17.

16. Gospel of Philip, 63, 32–64, 9.

17. Ibid., 59, 6–11.

18. Elisabeth Schüssler Fiorenza, "Word, Spirit, and Power: Women in Early Christian Communities," in *Women of Spirit*, eds. Rosemary Radford Ruether and Eleanor L. McLaughlin (New York: Simon and Schuster, 1979), 50.

19. Elaine Pagels, "The 'Mystery of Marriage' in the Gospel of Philip Revisited," in *The Future of Early Christianity*, ed. Birger A. Pearson (Minneapolis: Fortress Press, 1991), 449.

20. See also Karen L. King, "The Gospel of Mary Magdalene," in *Searching the Scriptures*, vol. 2, ed. Elisabeth Schüssler Fiorenza (New York: Crossroad, 1994), 616.

21. Audre Lorde, "The Uses of the Erotic," in *Weaving the Visions*, eds. Judith Plaskow and Carol Christ (San Francisco: Harper & Row, 1989), 208–13.

22. Gospel of Philip, 58, 34–59, 6.

23. King, "The Gospel of Mary Magdalene," 631 n. 42.

24. Manichaean Psalm Book, II 192, 21–22.

25. Gospel of Philip, 63, 31–64, 9.

26. Pistis Sophia, I, 36–37.

27. Ibid., II, 72.

28. The following sections of Pistis Sophia are referred to in this paragraph: II, 83; II, 97; II, 98; III, 108.

29. Acts of Philip, II, 81.

30. Acts of Peter, BG 8502, 4.

31. Gospel of Mary, 5:1–7:6. This text is based on the translations of the Coptic and Greek in Karen L. King, *The Gospel of Mary of Magdala: Jesus and the First Woman Apostle* (Santa Rosa, CA: Polebridge Press, 2003), 14–16.

32. Gospel of Mary, 9:30–10:14. Text based on translations of the Coptic and Greek in King, *The Gospel of Mary of Magdala*, 17–18.

33. King, "The Gospel of Mary Magdalene," 616.

Chapter Four: The Women Did Not Flee

1. Elisabeth Schüssler Fiorenza, in *Memory of Her: A Feminist Theological Reconstruction of Christian Origins*, 10th anniversary ed. (New York: Crossroad, 1994), 142.

2. Gloria Steinem, "A Great Woman Who Was Everywoman," *New York Times*, July 21, 2001, p. A27.

3. Judith Plaskow, "Anti-Judaism in Feminist Christian Interpretation," in *Searching the Scriptures*, vol. 1, ed. Elisabeth Schüssler Fiorenza (New York: Crossroad, 1997), 119–20, 123–24.

4. Eileen Schuller, "Women in the Dead Sea Scrolls," in *Methods of Investigation of the Dead Sea Scrolls and the Khirbet Qumran Site*, ed. Michael O. Wise (New York: Academy of Sciences, 1994), 115–31.

5. Josephus, *Jewish War* 4.504–6; see also 538–44.

6. See M. *Sotah* 3:4 and m. *Nedarim* 4:3.

7. Tal Ilan, "Paul and Pharisee Women," in *On the Cutting Edge: The Study of Women in Biblical Worlds*, eds. Jane Schaberg and Alice Bach (New York: Continuum, 2003), 92–94.

8. Mary Rose D'Angelo, "Reconstructing 'Real' Women in Gospel Literature: The Case of Mary Magdalene," in *Women and Christian Origins*, eds. Ross Kraemer and Mary Rose D'Angelo (Oxford: Oxford University Press, 1999), 122–25.

9. Elisabeth Schüssler Fiorenza, *Jesus: Miriam's Child, Sophia's Prophet* (New York: Continuum, 1994), 90.

10. Alan Segal, *Rebecca's Children* (Cambridge, MA: Harvard University Press, 1986), 71.

11. See, for example, the widely read views of John Dominic Crossan in *Jesus: A Revolutionary Biography* (San Francisco: HarperSanFrancisco, 1994).

12. Tacitus, *Ann.* 6.19; Suetonius, *Tiberias* 61.

13. Josephus, *Jewish War* 2. 253, 305–8; Philo, *In Flaccum* 72.

14. Pliny, *Letters* 10.96–97.

15. Suetonius, *Augustus* 13.1–2; Tacitus, *Ann.* 6.29; Petronius, *Satyricon* 111–12; Horace, *Epistle* 1.16.48.

16. Josephus, *Jewish War* 4. 317; 3. 377; *Antiquities* 4. 264–65; 4. 202.

17. m. *Sanh.* 6:5–6; t. *Sanh.* 9.8.

18. Josephus, *Jewish War* 2. 163.

19. Schüssler Fiorenza, *Jesus*, 90.

Chapter Five: Mary Magdalene as Successor to Jesus

1. C. H. Dodd, *More New Testament Studies* (Manchester: Manchester University Press, 1968), 115.

2. For these scenes in rabbinic literature, see b. *Sanh.* 68a; *Avot of Rabbi Nathan* [A] 25; *Semahot* 9:2; p. *Shab.* 5b; and Ber. R. 25, 1 Ezek 24:16.

3. C. L. Blockson, *The Underground Railroad* (New York: Hippocrene, 1994), 337–38.

4. Josephus, *Jewish War* 5.

5. Joan E. Taylor, "The Women 'Priests' of Philo's De Vita Contemplativa: Reconstructing the Therapeutae," in *On the Cutting Edge: The Study of Women in Biblical Worlds*, eds. Jane Schaberg, Alice Bach, and Esther Fuchs (New York: Continuum, 2004), 102–22.

6. Jerome Neyrey, "The Sociology of Secrecy and the Fourth Gospel," in *What is John?* vol. 2, ed. Fernando Segovia (Atlanta: Scholars Press, 1998), 104–5.

7. Sandra Schneiders, *Written That You May Believe: Encountering Jesus in the Fourth Gospel* (New York: Crossroad, 1999), 99.

8. Adele Reinhartz, *Befriending the Beloved Disciple: A Jewish Reading of the Gospel of John* (New York: Continuum, 2001), 111.

9. Mary Rose D'Angelo, "Reconstructing 'Real' Women in Gospel Literature: The Case of Mary Magdalene," *Women and Christian Origins*, eds. Ross Kraemer and Mary Rose D'Angelo (Oxford: Oxford University Press, 1999), 120, 136.

10. Tania Modeleski, *Feminism Without Women* (New York: Routledge, 1991), 7–9.

11. Epiphanius, *Adv. Haeres.* 26.13.228.

12. D'Angelo, "Reconstructing," 112.

13. Pheme Perkins, "'I Have Seen the Lord' (John 20:18): Women Witnesses to the Resurrection," *Interpretation* 46 (1992): 40–41.

14. Mary Rose D'Angelo, "(Re)presentations of Women in the Gospels: John and Mark," in *Women and Christian Origins*, 137.

15. J. Louis Martyn, "We Have Found Elijah," in *The Gospel of John in Christian History* (New York: Paulist Press, 1979), 9–54. Much of this discussion of the patterns in John 1 is working with Martin's observations and proposals.

16. Origen, *Contra Celsum* 2.55.

About the Authors

Melanie Johnson-DeBaufre is a Christian Testament scholar and professor of early Christianity at Drew Theological and Graduate Schools in Madison, New Jersey. She has a master's and doctorate at Harvard Divinity School and is ordained in the American Baptist Churches, USA. The author of *Jesus Among Her Children: Q, Eschatology, and the Construction of Christian Origins* (Harvard University Press, 2006), Dr. Johnson-DeBaufre researches the social-political world and textual traditions of the earliest Christianities (the historical Jesus, Q, and Pauline communities) and examines how contemporary discussions about Christianity imagine and make claims to these traditions. She is an editor and contributor to the *Journal of Feminist Studies in Religion* and *Walk in the Ways of Wisdom: Essays in Honor of Elisabeth Schüssler Fiorenza* (Trinity Press International, 2003). In her research, teaching, and speaking, she is interested in the uses of the Bible in public debates, and in creating opportunities for learning and exchange among feminist biblical scholars, religious communities, and social activists.

Jane Schaberg is professor of Religious Studies and Women's Studies at the University of Detroit Mercy. She has a master's degree from Columbia University in systematic theology, and a PhD from Union Theological Seminary NYC in biblical studies. Among her publications is *The Illegitimacy of Jesus: A Feminist Theological Interpretation of the New Testament Infancy Narratives*, which will appear in a 20th anniversary edition with additions by Phoenix Sheffield Press in 2006. She is an editor and contributor to *On the Cutting Edge: Women in Biblical Worlds, Essays in Honor of Elisabeth Schüssler Fiorenza* (Continuum, 2003). She lectures widely and enjoys varied audiences. Her current work is a memoir, with her goddaughter Carolyn Johnson and her godson Anthony Martin, of life on and beyond Seventeenth Street in downtown Detroit.